Practical English 1

second edition

Practical English 1

second edition

TIM HARRIS

Illustrated by **ALLAN ROWE**

HEINLE
CENGAGE Learning

Australia • Brazil • Japan • Korea • Mexico • Singapore • Spain • United Kingdom • United States

Practical English 1, Second Edition

For permission to use material from this text or product, submit all requests online at **cengage.com/permissions** Further permissions questions can be mailed to **permissionrequest@cengage.com**

Library of Congress Catalog Card Number: 85-81762
ISBN 13: 978-0-15-570912-6
ISBN 10: 0-15-570912-7

Heinle
20 Channel Center
Boston, MA 02210
USA

Cengage Learning products are represented in Canada by Nelson Education, Ltd.

Visit Heinle online at **elt.heinle.com**
Visit our corporate website at **www.cengage.com**

Printed in the United States of America
34 35 36 37 38 39 40 12 11 10 09

Preface

to the Second Edition

Practical English has been revised and expanded, taking into account the latest developments in English language teaching. Here's what to look for in the Second Edition:

- **A more balanced approach.** The new edition gives students more opportunities to perform language functions as they learn the basic structures. They practice asking for and giving information, expressing likes and dislikes, making suggestions, agreeing and disagreeing, and so on.

- **Greater emphasis on interactive communication and personal expression.** New illustrations and exercises provide many additional opportunities for students to ask each other questions and express themselves on a variety of subjects.

- **More writing activities.** These include composition exercises designed to help students make the transition from writing sentences to writing paragraphs. Picture stories and personal questions on a given topic provide material for writing short compositions.

- **Addition of two review chapters to book 1 and book 2.** These chapters contain humorous dialogues and stories, and a variety of exercises that reinforce and expand on material presented earlier. Tests are also included to help evaluate the students' progress.

- **Introduction of a split edition.** A six-volume split edition of *Practical English* is now available in addition to the regular three-volume series. The split edition is ideal for short courses offering fewer hours of instruction.

Preface
to the First Edition

Practical English is a comprehensive series designed to teach English as a second or a foreign language. Students who use *Practical English* will learn all four language skills—listening, speaking, reading, and writing—from the beginning. In book 1 the emphasis is on oral communication; books 2 and 3 give increased attention to reading and writing. Supplementary materials include workbooks and tape cassettes for additional writing and listening practice, and instructor's manuals containing useful teaching suggestions and answers to all text and workbook exercises.

In writing *Practical English* our overriding concern has been to create material that is appropriate for adult and secondary-school students. This has been accomplished by using a broad range of characters and real-life situations to teach the language. The grammar is presented in a way that takes advantage of the greater maturity and reasoning power of students at the adult and secondary levels. Structural items are demonstrated, rather than taught in the form of rules to be memorized. Students are encouraged to form their own conclusions based on the examples given. The idea is to get the students involved in a creative learning process that enables them to develop their grammatical intuition.

There is no question that mature students need a sound working knowledge of grammar if they are to be confident and creative in using their new language. However, it is not enough to master the grammatical structures of English. Students must be able to relate the language to their own personal needs and interests. For this reason, *Practical English* includes a number of open-ended exercises that allow for free expression.

The free-response questions in the first book give students the opportunity to talk about themselves using simple, straightforward English. Once they have progressed beyond the elementary level, they are ready for more creative language practice. In books 2 and 3, each chapter has a special section called "One Step Further" with discussion topics such as sports, hobbies, music, cinema, travel, dating, and marriage. Ideas for sketches have been provided to give additional opportunities for free expression. The general themes are familiar to students, as they are drawn from the dialogues and stories in the text.

Among the outstanding features of *Practical English* are the following:

1. **Preliminary oral work**. We feel that beginning students should have the opportunity to hear and use the target language before they open their books. Direct interaction between instructor and students makes it possible to engage in meaningful communication from the first day of class. In the instructor's manual we have included detailed, easy-to-follow suggestions for introducing new structures orally, without the aid of a text. Instructors can adapt these techniques to suit their own teaching styles.

2. **Illustrated situations**. As soon as a given item has been introduced orally, students should encounter it in a situational context. This ordinarily takes the form of an illustrated situation accompanied by a short reading or story. The students are asked to describe the illustration in their own words before hearing the accompanying text. This oral activity helps students retain what they have already learned

and serves as a lead-in for the text, which has been specially written to teach the new structure. The instructor may read the text to the class or have students listen to it from a tape. Then they answer questions based on the text, while looking at the illustration. The students respond to what they see and hear without referring to a text, just as they would in actual conversation.

3. **Dialogues.** Each chapter in the books is divided into three units. Sections A and B generally begin with an illustrated situation featuring a basic grammatical structure. The structure appears next in a situational dialogue with pictures to help students understand the meaning of the statements. As with the illustrated situations, the dialogues may be read to the class or heard from a tape. When students have had sufficient practice in listening to a particular dialogue and repeating the statements, the instructor may ask comprehension questions based on the text. The dialogues are short and well defined, so that students can learn them quickly and act out the parts. As an alternative to acting, students may be asked to reconstruct a given dialogue by referring only to the pictures.

4. **Oral exercises.** The illustrated situations and dialogues are followed by oral exercises or drills, which give further practice in using the same structures. The various exercise techniques include transformation, question-and-answer, substitution, and sentence completion. The exercises are relatively simple at the beginning of each chapter, becoming more difficult toward the end. They are designed to help students acquire language concepts, as well as accuracy and fluency in speaking.

5. **Reading passages.** Section C of most chapters opens with an illustrated reading passage that combines new structures with previous material in a natural context. The passage is followed by a series of comprehension questions that can be done orally or in written form, in class or at home. The reading passage provides a useful context for class conversation and, in many instances, for sketches.

By the time students come to the reading passage they will generally have sufficient confidence in using the new structures to do a sketch based on the story. Acting-out situations should be encouraged whenever possible, as this gives students a chance to be spontaneous and creative in using their new language. Accordingly, the major portion of each book is given over to illustrated situations, dialogues, and reading passages, all of which promote dramatization and interaction on the part of students.

6. **Review drills.** In addition to the reading passage, section C contains review drills and exercises designed to reinforce and consolidate what has been learned in sections A and B. The exercises in section C are generally more difficult than those in sections A and B and may be assigned as homework.

Section C also has lists of new vocabulary and expressions, followed by pronunciation exercises. The pronunciation exercises focus on sounds that have proved difficult for students of English as a second or a foreign language.

7. **Grammar frames.** At the end of section C there are grammar frames that summarize the basic structures taught in the chapter, confirming what students have learned through concrete observation and practice. The grammar frames allow students to review at home the structural material they have been learning in class.

Students using *Practical English* will find it much easier to assimilate the basic grammar points as they encounter each item in a variety of contexts.

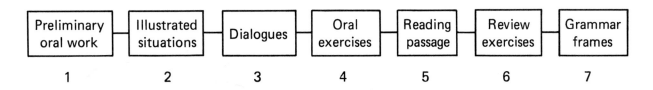

Preliminary oral work	Illustrated situations	Dialogues	Oral exercises	Reading passage	Review exercises	Grammar frames
1	2	3	4	5	6	7

Each volume of *Practical English* is accompanied by a workbook, called *Writing Practical English.* The lessons in the workbook are closely coordinated with the lessons in the text. They provide additional writing practice in using the same grammatical structures and vocabulary.

There are also cassettes for each volume of the text—a set of three tapes per volume. The cassettes include the dialogues, stories, and pronunciation exercises in *Practical English.* They give students an opportunity to hear English spoken by native speakers representing all age groups.

The teaching methods used in this series will provide students with a good functional knowledge of grammar. Having each structure demonstrated in a variety of contexts enables students to make generalizations about the language that are reliable and useful. They develop a "language sense," a feeling for words that carries over into their daily use of English. As a result, they can say what they want to say and have it stay with them outside the classroom.

To our families—
and two very special Cariocas

ACKNOWLEDGMENTS

We wish to thank Ann Karat, Alisa Blatt, Tony Harris, Bennetta Hamilton, and Estela Cruz
for their valuable assistance in the preparation of this series.
And special thanks to Kern Krapohl for contributing some of the best stories.

Contents

CHAPTER ONE

PETER: Hello. What's your name?

MARIA: My name's Maria.

PETER: My name's Peter.

MARIA: Nice to meet you, Peter.

BARBARA: Good morning.

TINO: Good morning. How are you?

BARBARA: I'm fine. And you?

TINO: Fine, thank you.

This is John Bascomb.

He's a banker.

This is Maria Miranda.

She's a doctor.

This is Peter Smith.

He's a businessman.

This is Anne Jones.

She's a secretary.

This is Nancy Paine.

She isn't a doctor.

She's a pilot.

This is Otis Jackson.

He isn't a businessman.

He's an artist.

This is Ula Hackey.

She isn't a secretary.

She's a movie star.

This is Nick Vitakis.

He isn't a banker.

He's a mechanic.

FRED: Who's that?

BARNEY: Her name is Nancy Paine.

FRED: Is she a mechanic?

BARNEY: No, she isn't.

FRED: What is she?

BARNEY: She's a pilot.

FRED: What's his name?

BARNEY: Otis Jackson.

FRED: Is he a pilot, too?

BARNEY: No, he isn't. He's
                an artist.

a   1. What's this?

It's a book.

2. What's this?

It's a chair.

3. What's this?

_____ bottle.

4. What's this?

_____ hat.

5. Is this a clock?

Yes, it is.

6. Is this a table?

Yes, it is.

7. Is this a book?
What is it?

No, it isn't.
It's a newspaper.

8. Is this a bottle?
What is it?

No, it isn't.
_____ glass.

9. Is this a clock?
What is it?

_____.
_____ watch.

10. Is this a hat?
What is it?

_____.
_____ coat.

b

1. What's this?
   It's a rabbit.

2. What's this?
   It's a chicken.

3. What's _____?
   It's a pear.

4. What's that?

   It's a bird.

5. What's that?

   It's a dog.

6. What's _____?

   It's an apple.

7. Is that a cat?   Yes, it is.

8. Is this a dog?

   No, it isn't.

   It's a _____.

9. Is _____ an apple?

   No, it isn't.
   It's a _____.

10. Is _____ an apple?   Yes, it is.

c

1. What are these?
   They're flowers.

2. What are these?
   They're cards.

3. What are _____?
   They're rabbits.

4. What are those?   They're chickens.

5. What are those?   They're cats.

6. What are _____?   They're dogs.

7. Are these rabbits?
   Yes, they are.

8. Are those pears?   Yes, they are.

9. Are _____ cats?
   No, they aren't.
   They're _____.

10. Are _____ apples?
    No, they aren't.
    They're _____.

The cat is <u>under</u> the table.

    The ball is <u>in front of</u> the cat.

The vase is <u>on</u> the table.

    The flower is <u>in</u> the vase.

The envelope is <u>on</u> the table.

    The envelope is <u>next to</u> the vase.

The bookcase is <u>behind</u> the table.

    The books are <u>in</u> the bookcase.

d 1. Where's the cat now?
It's _____ the table.

2. Where's the dog?
It's _____ the table.

3. Where's the vase?
It's _____ the floor.

4. Where's the flower?
It's _____ the vase.

5. Where's the envelope?
It's _____ the cat.

6. Where's the ball?
It's _____ the dog.

1

Ula Hackey is at the movies.

2

Otis is at the museum.

3

Mr. Bascomb is at the bank.

4

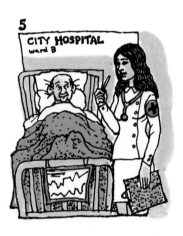

Nick is at the garage.

5

Maria is at the hospital.

6

Peter is at the office.

7

Nancy is at the airport.

8

Anne is at the post office.

9

Barney is at the gas station.

a *Replace with **he** or **she***.

1. Ula is at the movies.
   She's at the movies.
2. Otis is at the museum.
   He's at the museum.
3. Mr. Bascomb is at the bank.
4. Nick is at the garage.

5. Maria is at the hospital.
6. Peter is at the office.
7. Nancy is at the airport.
8. Anne is at the post office.
9. Barney is at the gas station.

b *Look at the pictures on page 10 and answer the following questions.*

1. Is Ula at the movies?
   Yes, she is.
2. Is Otis at the post office?
   No, he isn't. He's at the museum.
3. Is Mr. Bascomb at the hospital?
4. Is Nick at the garage?

5. Is Maria at the airport?
6. Is Peter at the office?
7. Is Nancy at the movies?
8. Is Anne at the bank?
9. Is Barney at the gas station?

c *Change the following sentences to the interrogative.*

Example: He is a banker.
         Is he a banker?

1. She is a pilot.
2. He is a taxi driver.
3. She is a doctor.
4. He is an artist.

5. He is a mechanic.
6. She is a secretary.
7. He is a businessman.
8. She is a movie star.

d *Complete with **a** or **an***.

Examples: It's _____ glass.   It's _____ egg.
           It's <u>a</u> glass.   It's <u>an</u> egg.

1. It's _____ tree.
2. It's _____ apple.
3. It's _____ car.

4. It's _____ bottle.
5. It's _____ orange.
6. It's _____ envelope.

7. It's _____ library.
8. It's _____ newspaper.
9. It's _____ airport.

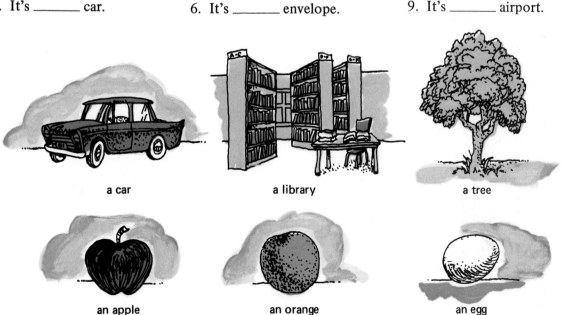

a car   a library   a tree

an apple   an orange   an egg

Note: *a* before consonant   *an* before a, e, i, o, u

e   *Complete the sentences.*

Example: Where's the bus stop? It's _____*at*_____ the corner.

1. Where's Barbara? She's _____ the bus stop.

2. Where's the truck? It's _____ the bus.

3. Where's the post office? It's _____ the garage.

4. Where's the tree? It's _____ the garage.

5. Where's the car? It's _____ the garage.

6. Where's Nick? He's _____ the car.

f   *Answer the following questions about the picture.*

Examples: Is the bus stop at the corner?
         Yes, it is.

         Is Barbara in the post office?
         No, she isn't. She's at the bus stop.

1. Is the truck behind the bus?
2. Is the post office next to the garage?
3. Is the tree behind the post office?
4. Is the car in front of the garage?
5. Is Nick in the car?

g *Complete the sentences as indicated.*

1. What's *this* ? It's *a hat* .

2. What's _____? It's _____ .

3. What's _____ ? It's _____ .

4. What's _____? It's _____ .

5. What are _____? They're _____ .

6. What are _____? They're _____ .

7. What are _____ ? They're _____ .

8. What are _____ ? They're _____

VOCABULARY

a	businessman	garage	mechanic	pilot	truck
airplane	bus stop	gas station	meet	post office	
airport		glass	movies		under
am	car	good morning	movie star	rabbit	
an	card		Mr.		vase
and	cat	hat	museum	secretary	
apple	chair	he	my	she	watch (n.)
are	chicken	hello			what
artist	clock	her	name (n.)	table	where
at	coat	his	newspaper	taxi driver	who
	corner	hospital	next to	thank you	
ball		how	nice	that	yes
bank	doctor		no	the	you
banker	dog	I	not	these	your
behind		in		they	
bird	egg	in front of	office	this	
book	envelope	is	on	those	
bookcase		it	orange	to	
bottle	fine			too	
bus	flower	library	pear	tree	

EXPRESSIONS

Hello. What's your name?   How are you?   Where's Barbara?

My name is Maria.   I'm fine, and you?   at the corner

Nice to meet you.   Fine, thank you.   at the movies

airplane

PRONOUNCE THESE WORDS CLEARLY

ey		æ	
n<u>a</u>me	bookc<u>a</u>se	c<u>a</u>t	<u>a</u>pple
v<u>a</u>se	airpl<u>a</u>ne	h<u>a</u>t	t<u>a</u>xi
t<u>a</u>ble	newsp<u>a</u>per	th<u>a</u>t	r<u>a</u>bbit
st<u>a</u>tion		gl<u>a</u>ss	mech<u>a</u>nic

TO BE Affirmative

He She It	's (is)	in the office.

Negative

He She It	isn't (is not) 's not	in the office.

Interrogative

Is	he she it	in the office?

Short Answers

Yes,	he she it	is.

No,	he she it	isn't.

Question with WHAT

What	's (is)	this? that?
	are	these? those?

SINGULAR AND PLURAL NOUNS

It	's (is)	a pear an apple.
They	're (are)	cards. flowers.

Question with WHERE

Where	's (is)	Mr. Bascomb?
	's (is)	the newspaper?
	are	the books?

PREPOSITIONS

He	's (is)	at in	the bank. his office.
It	's (is)	on under next to	the table.
They	're (are)	behind in front of	

Question with WHO

Who	's (is)	that?

Otis Jackson.

CHAPTER TWO

''To be'' with adjective

''To be'' with adjective and noun

Singular and plural nouns

Numbers 1–20

Time

WAITER: Excuse me. Are you a tourist?

TOURIST: Yes, I am.

WAITER: Are you English?

TOURIST: No, I'm not.

WAITER: What nationality are you?

TOURIST: I'm American.

a   *Answer the following questions about yourself.*

Example: Are you a businessman?
        Yes, I am.   OR   **No, I'm not.**

1. Are you Italian?
2. Are you an artist?
3. Are you rich?
4. Are you married?
5. Are you a tourist?
6. Are you hot?
7. Are you thirsty?
8. Are you happy?
9. Are you sad?
10. Are you cold?

happy   sad

PEDRO: Are you from the United States?

STEVE: Yes, we are. We're from Hollywood.

PEDRO: Are you movie stars?

STEVE: No, we aren't movie stars. We're students.

JUANITA: Who are they?

PEDRO: They're Americans. They're
           from Hollywood.

JUANITA: Are they movie stars?

PEDRO: No, they aren't. They're students.

b *Replace with* **you**, **we**, *or* **they**.

Example: <u>Barney and I</u> are friends.
        We're friends.

1. <u>Anne and Nancy</u> are Americans.
2. <u>You and Nancy</u> are from New York.
3. <u>Anne and Peter</u> are from Los Angeles.
4. <u>Anne and I</u> are friends.
5. <u>You and Nancy</u> are friends.
6. <u>You and I</u> are students.
7. <u>Those girls</u> are students.

c *Change the following sentences to the interrogative.*

Example: They're businessmen.
        Are they businessmen?

1. They're at a business meeting.
2. They're at the City Bank.
3. They're on Franklin Avenue.
4. We're on Main Street.
5. We're at the post office.
6. You're doctors.
7. You're from the hospital.

d *Change the following sentences to the negative.*

Example: You're movie stars.
        You aren't movie stars.

1. You're tourists.
2. You're from England.
3. You're rich.
4. We're happy.
5. We're businessmen.
6. They're pilots.
7. They're Americans.

e Tino is a waiter. He's tall and handsome. He isn't rich, but he's happy. Barbara is a secretary. She's short and blond. And she's beautiful. Barbara and Tino are good friends. They're from California.

1. Is Tino a businessman?
2. Is he short?
3. Is he handsome?
4. Is he rich?
5. Is Barbara a secretary?
6. Is she tall?
7. Is she blond?
8. Is she beautiful?
9. Are Barbara and Tino good friends?
10. Are they from New York?

f Natalya and Boris are Russian ballet dancers. They're from Moscow. They're very good dancers.

1. Are Natalya and Boris ballet dancers or movie stars?
2. Where are they from?
3. Are they good dancers?

g Sammy and Tammy are country singers. They're from Texas. They aren't very good singers. In fact, they're very bad.

1. Are Sammy and Tammy singers or dancers?
2. Where are they from?
3. Are they good singers?

This woman is fat.

That man is thin.

This bicycle is cheap.

That bicycle is expensive.

These women are young.

Those men are old.

These boys are dirty.

Those girls are clean.

a *Complete the sentences about the pictures above, using these adjectives:*
bad, clean, beautiful, hot, cheap, fat, rich, married, short.

1. Barbara ___*is beautiful*___ .   6. Tino _____ .

2. Mr. and Mrs. Bascomb _____ .   7. The pots _____ .

3. Mr. Twaddle _____ .   8. The guitar _____ .

4. Mrs. Brown _____ .   9. The apples _____ .

5. Albert _____ .

b *Answer the following questions as indicated.*

1. Is Barbara beautiful?
   Yes, she is.
2. Are Mr. and Mrs. Bascomb poor?
   No, they aren't. They're rich.
3. Is Mr. Twaddle tall?
4. Is Mrs. Brown married?

5. Is Albert thin?
6. Is Tino cold?
7. Are the pots clean?
8. Is the guitar expensive?
9. Are the apples good?

TINO: That's a beautiful red dress, Barbara.

BARBARA: Thank you, Tino. It's new.

TINO: Red is a good color for you.

BARBARA: Yes. It's my favorite color.

TINO: Are those new shoes?

BARBARA: Yes, they are. They're brand-new.

c   *Change the following sentences as indicated.*

Examples: That's a pretty dress.   This is a cheap hat.
          That dress is pretty.   **This hat is cheap.**

1. That's an old newspaper.   6. This is a bad apple.
2. This is a good book.   7. That's a beautiful tree.
3. That's an expensive coat.   8. That's a clean car.
4. This is a dirty glass.   9. This is a new bicycle.
5. That's an old chair.

d   *Change the above sentences from singular to plural.*

Examples: That's a pretty dress.   This is a cheap hat.
          Those are pretty dresses.   **These are cheap hats.**

NUMBERS

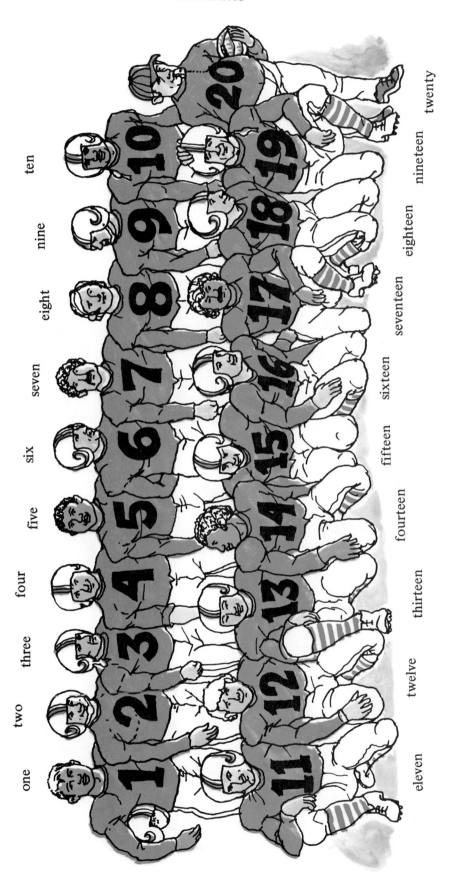

one two three four five six seven eight nine ten

eleven twelve thirteen fourteen fifteen sixteen seventeen eighteen nineteen twenty

e   What time is it?

A.

It's one o'clock.

B.

It's eight o'clock.

C.

It's three o'clock.

D.

E.

F.

G.

H.

I.

J.

K.

L.

Albert is with Mr. Watkins, his favorite teacher at the university.

ALBERT:	Who's that girl by the window?
MR. WATKINS:	It's Lúcia Mendes.
ALBERT:	She's very pretty. Is she a student?
MR. WATKINS:	Yes. She's a history student.
ALBERT:	Is Lúcia Mexican?
MR. WATKINS:	No, she isn't. She's Brazilian.

ALBERT:	What city is she from?
MR. WATKINS:	She's from Rio de Janeiro.
ALBERT:	Is that the capital of Brazil?
MR. WATKINS:	No. Brasília is the capital.

ALBERT:	What's Brasília like?
MR. WATKINS:	It's a beautiful modern city.

a   *Answer the following questions about the dialogue.*

1. Who's Albert with?
2. Is Mr. Watkins an intelligent man?
3. Who's the girl by the window?
4. Is she very pretty?
5. Is she American?
6. What nationality is she?
7. What city is she from?
8. Is Rio de Janeiro the capital of Brazil?
9. What is the capital of Brazil?
10. What's Brasília like?
11. What's the capital of your country?
12. What's your capital like?

b   *Ask and answer questions about the students in your class, as in the dialogue on page 27.*

Student A: Who's that boy/girl over there?

Student B: It's _____ .

Student A: Is he/she Mexican/Chinese/ French?

Student B: _____ .

Student A: What city is he/she from?

Student B: _____ .

c   *Complete the sentences with the correct form of the verb* **to be.**

1. Peter _____ at the office.
2. He _____ a young businessman.
3. Linda and I _____ at the university.
4. We _____ in the library.
5. It _____ a modern buliding.
6. Linda _____ next to the window.
7. She _____ a tall, thin girl.
8. It _____ very hot today.
9. I _____ thirsty.
10. _____ you thirsty, too?

d   *Change the following sentences from singular to plural.*

Examples: It's an old city.
            They're old cities.

            She's a young woman.
            They're young women.

1. It's an expensive car.
2. He's an old man.
3. She's an intelligent girl.
4. It's a modern building.
5. She's a good secretary.
6. He's a fine mechanic.
7. It's a new bus.
8. He's a young pilot.
9. She's a married woman.

e   *Answer the following questions as indicated.*

Example: Is Mr. Bascomb poor? (rich)
          No, he isn't. He's rich.

1. Is he stupid? (intelligent)
2. Is he sad? (happy)
3. Are Barbara and Tino married? (single)
4. Are they old? (young)
5. Is your car big? (small)
6. Is it expensive? (cheap)
7. Is it clean? (dirty)
8. Is Albert thin? (fat)
9. Is Sophia Loren French? (Italian)

Mr. Bascomb

Maria is at home. She's
in the living room.

Mr. Bascomb is at work.
He's in his office.

The children are at school.
They're in the classroom.

f   *Make questions as indicated.*

Examples: Maria is at home. _____*Is she*_____ in the living room?

The students are at the university. _____*Are they*_____ in the library?

1. Mr. Bascomb is at work. _____He's_____ in his office?

2. The children are at school. _____They're_____ in the classroom?

3. Barbara is on Maple Street. _____He's_____ at the bus stop?

4. Otis is at the museum. _____He's_____ with his friends?

5. The tourists are at the airport. _____They're_____ in the airplane?

6. Albert is at the university. _____He's_____ with Mr. Watkins?

7. Lúcia is in the classroom. _____He's_____ by the window?

8. The magazines are in the office. _____it's_____ on the desk?

9. The newspaper is in the living room. _____it's_____ on the table?

g   *Change the following sentences as indicated.*

Examples: She's an Italian movie star. (beautiful)
           She's a beautiful Italian movie star.

           They're German girls. (young)
           They're young German girls.

1. He's a young doctor. (fine)
2. It's a red dress. (expensive)
3. We're art students. (young)
4. She's a ballet dancer. (good)
5. They're school books. (old)
6. It's an English car. (new)
7. He's an American tourist. (rich)
8. They're office buildings. (modern)
9. It's a black umbrella. (small)

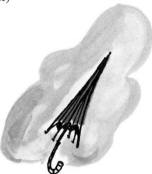

an umbrella

h *Complete the sentences.*

Example: Where's the book? It's ___*on*___ the desk.

1. Where's the teacher? He's _____ the desk.

2. Where's the wastebasket? It's _____ the desk.

3. Where's the newspaper? It's _____ the wastebasket.

4. Where's the chair? It's _____ the desk.

5. Where's the hat? It's _____ the chair.

6. Where's the umbrella? It's _____ the chair.

i *Answer the questions about the picture.*

Examples: Is the book on the desk?   Is the teacher in front of the desk?
          Yes, it is.   **No, he isn't. He's behind the desk.**

1. Is the wastebasket on the desk?
2. Is the newspaper in the wastebasket?
3. Is the chair behind the desk?
4. Is the hat on the floor?
5. Is the umbrella under the chair?

VOCABULARY

American	country singer	friend	married	sad	tourist
	cowboy	from	me	school	twelve
bad			meeting	seven	twenty
ballet	dancer	German	Mexican	seventeen	two
beautiful	desk	girl	modern	shoe	
bicycle	dirty	good	Mrs.	short	ugly
big	dress	guitar		singer	umbrella
black			nationality	single	university
blond	eight	handsome	new	six	
boy	eighteen	happy	nine	sixteen	very
brand-new	eleven	history	nineteen	small	
Brazilian	English	home		Spanish	waiter
building	excuse (v.)	hot	o'clock	student	wastebasket
business	expensive	hungry	old	stupid	we
			one		window
capital	fat	intelligent		tall	woman
cheap	favorite	Italian	poor	teacher	work
city	fifteen		pot	ten	
classroom	five	like	pretty	thin	young
clean (adj.)	floor	living room		thirsty	
cold	four		red	thirteen	
color	fourteen	magazine	rich	three	
country	French	man	Russian	time	

EXPRESSIONS

Excuse me.	What's it like?	at home	at school
What time is it?	brand-new	at work	over there

OPPOSITES

hot ≠ cold	big ≠ small	good ≠ bad	beautiful ≠ ugly
fat ≠ thin	old ≠ young	happy ≠ sad	intelligent ≠ stupid
short ≠ tall	old ≠ new	rich ≠ poor	expensive ≠ cheap

PRONOUNCE THESE WORDS CLEARLY			
ay		**i**	
time	pilot	this	city
like	library	big	window
fine	bicycle	rich	single
nice	behind	thin	chicken

STRESS AND INTONATION

Excuse me. Are you a tourist?

Yes, I am.

Are you English?

No, I'm not.

What nationality are you?

I'm American.

Is John a doctor?

No, he isn't. He's a banker.

What city is he from?

He's from Wickam City.

Is your name Barney or Fred?

My name is Barney.

TO BE   Affirmative

He She It	's (is)	
I	'm (am)	in the library.
You We They	're (are)	

Negative

He She It	isn't (is not) 's not	
I	'm not (am not)	in the library.
You We They	aren't (are not) 're not	

Interrogative

Is	he she it	
Am	I	in the library?
Are	you we they	

Short answers

	he she it	is.
Yes,	I	am.
	you we they	are.

	he she it	isn't.
No,	I	'm not.
	you we they	aren't.

ADJECTIVES AND WORD ORDER

The city	is	beautiful.
The buildings	are	modern.

It's	a beautiful city.
They're	modern buildings.

It's a beautiful modern city.

They're beautiful modern buildings.

PLURALS

bus	buses	city	cities
watch	watches	library	libraries
glass	glasses	secretary	secretaries

Irregular

man	men
woman	women
child	children

TIME

What time is it?

It's five o'clock.

NUMBERS 1–20

1 one	6 six	11 eleven	16 sixteen
2 two	7 seven	12 twelve	17 seventeen
3 three	8 eight	13 thirteen	18 eighteen
4 four	9 nine	14 fourteen	19 nineteen
5 five	10 ten	15 fifteen	20 twenty

PREPOSITIONS

Albert is	with	his favorite teacher.
Lúcia is	from	Rio de Janeiro.
She's	by	the window.

CHAPTER THREE

Close your book.

Stand up.

Go to the blackboard.

Write your name.

Sit down.

Be quiet.

Don't talk.

Don't write on the table.

Don't open the window.

Don't eat in class.

Don't leave the room.

Don't laugh.

Hello, Johnnie. Come with <u>me</u>.

Oh, this bottle! Please open <u>it</u>.

There's Barbara and Tino.
Let's talk with <u>them</u>.

Peter is a very good dancer. Look at <u>him</u>.

Come and sit with <u>us</u>, Peter.

There's Alice. Go and talk with <u>her</u>.

OBJECT
PRONOUNS

Look at Peter.	Look at him.
Look at Maria.	Look at her.
Look at Barbara and Tino.	Look at them.
Look at Johnnie and me.	Look at us.
Look at the clock.	Look at it.

a *Make commands as indicated.*

Example: Peter is a very good dancer.
Look at him.

1. Barbara is beautiful tonight.
2. Albert is very happy.
3. The cat is hungry.
4. Those girls are very tall.
5. Tino and I are good dancers.
6. Alice is a bad dancer.
7. Johnnie is sad.
8. That clock is old.
9. These flowers are very pretty.

b *Change the following sentences as indicated.*

Example: Sit with Johnnie and me. *Sit with us.*

1. Close the door. Please close it
2. Open the windows. please open it
3. Talk to Mr. Bascomb. Let's talk with them
4. Listen to Barbara and me. look at he is beautful to night.
5. Repeat the question. Please don't laugh
6. Sit with Alice. Go and talk with her.
7. Dance with Peter. Look at him
8. Look at those girls. Go and talk with her
9. Listen to Maria. look at her.

Mrs. Brown is a housewife. She's in the kitchen with her children, Jimmy and Linda.

c   *Ask and answer questions about the objects in the picture.*

Example 1: cards   Example 2: pots
Student A: **Where are the cards?**   Student A: **Where are the pots?**
Student B: **They're on the floor.**   Student B: **They're on the wall.**

1. cups   4. flowers   7. glasses
2. pots   5. magazines   8. oranges
3. books   6. candles   9. dishes

MR. BASCOMB: Good morning, Barbara.

BARBARA: Good morning, Mr. Bascomb.
Here's a message from
Mr. Smith.

MR. BASCOMB: Ah, yes. Please call him.
Tell him the meeting
is at ten o'clock.

BARBARA: Yes, Mr. Bascomb.

MR. BASCOMB: And bring me a sandwich,
please. I'm hungry.

BARBARA: Yes, sir.

Call <u>Mr. Smith</u>.   Call <u>him</u>.
Ask <u>Mrs. Golo</u>.   Ask <u>her</u>.
Answer <u>the students</u>.   Answer <u>them</u>.
Call <u>Barbara and me</u>.   Call <u>us</u>.
Open <u>the window</u>.   Open <u>it</u>.

---

a *Complete the following sentences.*

Example: Mr. Bascomb is hungry. Bring ___*him*___ a sandwich.

1. Anne is in the hospital. Take ___her___ these flowers.

2. Mr. and Mrs. Golo are in France. Write ___me___ a letter.

3. We're thirsty. Bring ___him___ a bottle of Coca-Cola.

4. Jimmy is in class. Take ___Tell them___ this message.

5. Mrs. Brown is here. Give ___him___ those magazines.

6. The children are hungry. Bring ___me___ the large red apples.

7. Albert is here. Give ___Tell them___ your telephone number.

8. Barbara is at home. Take ___her___ this book.

9. We're in the kitchen. Bring ___us___ the glasses.

b *Make negative commands.*

Example: Bring us the glasses.
    Don't bring us the glasses.

1. Give them the newspaper.
2. Take her the magazines.
3. Write me a letter.
4. Give him a postcard.
5. Bring us the dictionary.
6. Take him a book.
7. Give her the envelopes.
8. Bring me the bottle.
9. Tell them the answer.

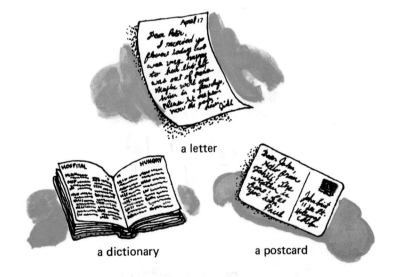

a letter

a dictionary   a postcard

twenty-one

twenty-two

twenty-three

twenty-four

twenty-five

twenty-six

twenty-seven

twenty-eight

twenty-nine

thirty

thirty-one

thirty-two

forty

forty-one

fifty

sixty

seventy

eighty

ninety

one hundred

MR. BASCOMB: How old is that lamp?

SALESMAN: It's ninety-eight years old.

MR. BASCOMB: How much is it?

SALESMAN: It's one hundred and twenty-five dollars.

MR. BASCOMB: That's a good price. Here you are, young man.

SALESMAN: Thank you, sir. Have a nice day.

c   *Answer the following questions as indicated.*

Examples: How old is the lamp?
          It's ninety-eight years old.

          How much is it?
          It's one hundred and twenty-five dollars.

1. How old is the clock?
2. How much is it?
3. How old is the chair?
4. How much is it?
5. How old are the guns?
6. How much are they?
7. How old is the table?
8. How much is it?
9. How old is the phonograph?
10. How much is it?
11. How old are the cups?
12. How much are they?

What time is it?

It's six o'clock.

It's fifteen minutes past eight.
It's (a) quarter past eight.

It's seven o'clock.

It's thirty minutes past eight.
It's half past eight.

It's ten minutes past seven.
It's seven ten.

It's fifteen minutes to ten.
It's (a) quarter to ten.

It's twenty minutes past seven.
It's seven twenty.

It's five minutes to ten.

What time is it?

It's noon.

It's midnight.

Morning is from
midnight to noon.

Afternoon is
from noon to six.

Evening is from
six to midnight.

a *Answer the following questions about the dialogue.*

1. Why is Mrs. Golo worried?
2. What's her address?
3. Is her house far from the post office?
4. Is the post office on Lime Street?

5. Is it a big fire or a little one?
6. Is Mrs. Golo in the house now?
7. Is it dangerous?

b *Make commands, using a suitable verb with each of the following words.*

Examples: exercise
                Read/write/repeat the exercise.

Mrs. Golo
Ask/answer/listen to Mrs. Golo.

1. lesson
2. book
3. door

4. Maria
5. magazine
6. window

7. question
8. Mr. Smith
9. letter

c *Make commands as indicated.*

Examples: These glasses are dirty. (wash)
                Wash them.

Maria isn't ready. (wait for)
Wait for her.

1. The door is open. (close)
2. There's Linda. (talk to)
3. Mr. and Mrs. Bascomb are in France. (write to)
4. Albert is at home. (call)

5. I'm your friend. (listen to)
6. Here's Mrs. Golo. (ask)
7. Those cats are hungry. (look at)
8. Peter is a very good dancer. (dance with)

d *Ask and answer questions about the picture on page 51. Use **between, next to** and **across . . . from** in your answers.*

Example 1: **the State Bank/City Park**
Student A: **Where's the State Bank?**
Student B: **It's across the street from Plummer Park.**

Example 2: **the Rex Theater/Mom's Cafe**
Student C: **Where's the Rex Theater?**
Student D: **It's next to Mom's Cafe.**

Example 3: **the barber shop**/the flower shop and the supermarket
Student E: **Where's the barber shop?**
Student F: **It's between the flower shop and the supermarket.**

1. **the church**/City Park
2. **the parking lot**/the supermarket and the Grand Hotel
3. **the flower shop**/the barber shop
4. **the drug store**/the church and the gas station
5. **the Grand Hotel**/Olson's Department Store
6. **the gas station**/the drug store
7. **Mom's Cafe**/the Rex Theater and the State Bank
8. **the book store**/the post office
9. **the supermarket**/the church

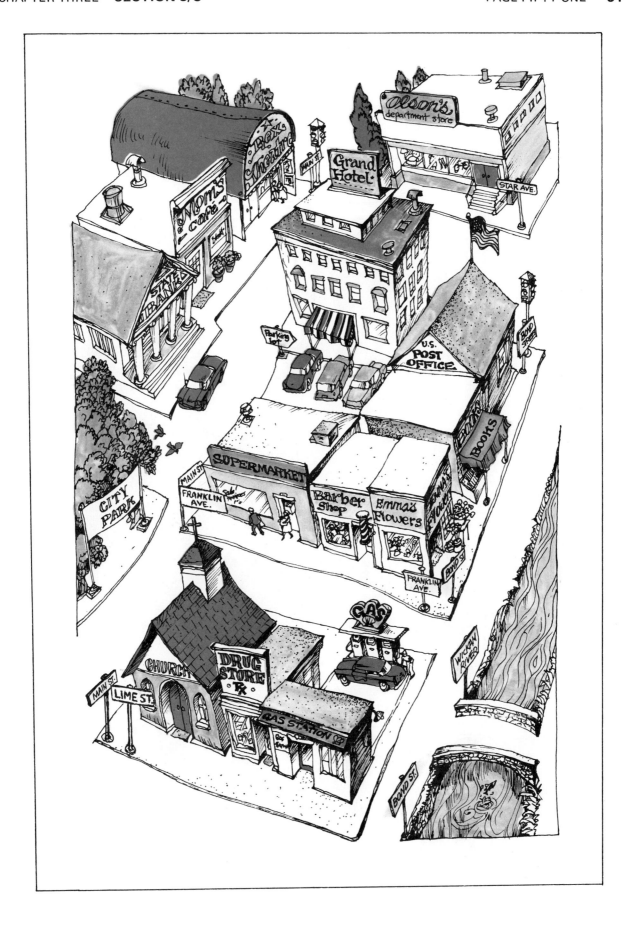

e *Look at the pictures and write the correct command for each one.*

Give me your money!   Dance with me!   Take me to the airport!
Don't worry!   Don't sit down!   Don't leave me!
Eat your dinner!   Don't touch me!   Answer the phone!

VOCABULARY

across	dictionary	housewife	noon	seventy
address (n.)	dinner		now	shelf
afternoon	dish	immediately	number	sir
ah	do		nurse	sit
all	dollar	kitchen		sixty
answer	door		of	stand
ask	down	lamp	oh	street
away	drugstore	large	one hundred	supermarket
		laugh	open	
barber shop	each	leave	outside	take
blackboard	eat	lesson		talk
book store	eighty	let	parking lot	telephone
bring	emergency	letter	past	them
	evening	light	phonograph	there
call		listen	please	thirty
cafe	father	little	postcard	tonight
candle	fifty	look (v.)	price	touch
church	fire		put	
class	fire department	ma'am		up
close (v.)	forty	match (n.)	quarter	us
Coca-Cola		message	question	
coffee	give	midnight		wait (v.)
come	go	minute	read	wall
cup	gun	money	ready	wash
		morning	repeat	with
dance (v.)	here	much	right	worry
dangerous	him		room	write
day	hotel	near		
department store	house	ninety	sandwich	year

EXPRESSIONS

ah	Here you are.	Let's talk.	Don't worry.	My house is on fire.
all right	How much is it?	Have a nice day.	Dinner's ready.	It's hot in here.
right away				

PRONOUNCE THESE WORDS CLEARLY

e		iy	
men	yes	he	meet
desk	seven	she	tree
them	letter	we	street
next	envelope	me	these

PRONUNCIATION

s

hats	pilots	cups
coats	students	pots
books	trucks	clocks
lamps	streets	desks

The books and lamps are on the desk.
Give Otis the rabbits and cats.

z

apples	boys	pens
pears	girls	letters
flowers	tables	cards
candles	chairs	bottles

Talk to those boys and girls.
Read those letters and magazines.

iz

vases	buses	watches
glasses	nurses	messages
dishes	matches	houses
oranges	dresses	addresses

The sandwiches and oranges are for the nurses.
Give them the glasses and dishes, too.

nurses

Those cars, buses, and trucks are new.
Please wash these cups, bottles, and dishes.
The pilots are with the doctors and nurses.

IMPERATIVE

Close the door!	
Open the window!	

Negative Imperative

Don't	close the door!
	open the window!

With Noun Objects

Look at	Peter. Maria. Barbara and Tino. Johnnie and me. the clock.

With Object Pronouns

Look at	him. her. them. us. it.

With Two Objects

Give	Jimmy Linda the children Albert and me the dog	an apple.

With Object Pronouns

Give	him her them us it	an apple.

Question with HOW MUCH

How much	is the watch?
	are the books?

It's twenty-five dollars.
They're ten dollars.

Question with HOW OLD

How old	is Barbara?
	are the chairs?

She's twenty-four years old.
They're fifteen years old.

What time is it?	It's	six seven	o'clock.
		ten minutes twenty minutes	past seven.
		(a) quarter half	past eight.
		(a) quarter five minutes	to ten.

NUMBERS 21–100

21	twenty-one	26	twenty-six	31	thirty-one	60	sixty
22	twenty-two	27	twenty-seven	32	thirty-two	70	seventy
23	twenty-three	28	twenty-eight	40	forty	80	eighty
24	twenty-four	29	twenty-nine	41	forty-one	90	ninety
25	twenty-five	30	thirty	50	fifty	100	one hundred

CHAPTER FOUR

Review

a   *Answer the following questions about the dialogue.*

1. Where is Mr. Wilson?
2. What time is it?
3. Who is Miss Tracy?
4. What is the dentist's name?
5. How are Mr. Wilson's teeth?
6. Where is the aspirin?
7. What is aspirin good for?

8. Where is the telephone?
9. Is the call for Miss Tracy?
10. Is Dr. Molar busy?
11. Is Mr. Wilson in good hands?
12. How much is Mr. Wilson's dental bill?
13. What is dental floss good for?
14. Is Miss Tracy a good nurse?

b   *Answer the following questions about yourself.*

1. How are your teeth?
2. Is your dentist like Dr. Molar?
3. What is your dentist's name?
4. Where is his/her office?
5. Is your dentist cheap or expensive?
6. Are you afraid when you are at the dentist's?
7. Is sugar good or bad for your teeth?

c   *Now write your name, address, telephone number, and occupation.*

d *Ask and answer questions about the pictures.*

1. A: **Where are Joe and Eddie?**
   B: **They're at the park.**

   A: **Are they businessmen?**
   B: **No, they aren't. (They're bums.)**

   A: **Are they hot or cold?**
   B: **They're cold.**

2. C: **Where's the cat?**
   D: **It's in the tree.**

   C: **Is it fat or thin?**
   D: **It's fat.**

   C: **Is it happy?**
   D: **Yes, it is.**

3. _This is_ ___ Maria?
   Are they ___ a doctor or a nurse?
   Your're ___ ugly?

4. _This is_ ___ Nick?
   Your're ___ a mechanic?
   _____ old or young?

5. _They are_ ___ Barbara and Anne?
   Are they ___ teachers or secretaries?
   They are ___ busy?

6. _____ Tino?
   _____ banker?
   _____ tall or short?

7. _Where is_____ the clock?
   _it is_____ big or small?
   _it's_____ old?

8. _Where's_____ the apples?
   _Are they_____ red or green?
   _They're_____ small?

9. _Where's_____ the woman?
   _Is it_____ young or old?
   _He's isn't_____ happy?

10. _They are_____ the boys?
    _They're_____ friends?
    _Are they_____ clean or dirty?

11. _Where are_____ Mr. and Mrs. Bascomb?
    _Are they_____ rich or poor?
    _They are_____ afraid?

12. _Where's_____ the Mercedes?
    _Is it_____ black or white?
    _it's_____ cheap?

e *Change the following sentences from singular to plural.*

Examples: That's an old bicycle.   This glass is clean.
            Those are old bicycles.   **These glasses are clean.**

1. That's an ugly building.   6. This is a big orange.
2. This is a cheap watch.   7. This window is dirty.
3. This dress is beautiful.   8. That boy is intelligent.
4. That hat is expensive.   9. That's a dangerous woman.
5. That's an old bicycle.

f *Make negative commands.*

Example: Listen to <u>Dr. Pasto</u>.
           Don't listen to <u>him</u>.

1. Call <u>Mrs. Golo</u>.   6. Open <u>the window</u>.
2. Read <u>this book</u>.   7. Ask <u>Maria</u>.
3. Look at <u>those men</u>.   8. Take <u>these apples</u>.
4. Sit with <u>Linda and me</u>.   9. Wait for <u>Peter and me</u>.
5. Talk to <u>Albert</u>.

g *Answer the following questions about yourself.*

1. Are you hungry?
2. What is your favorite fruit?
3. Are oranges cheap or expensive?
4. Are apples good for you? Coca-cola?
5. How much is a bottle of Coca-cola?
6. How is your family?
7. Is your family at home now?
8. Where are your friends?
9. Where is your house/apartment?
10. What color is your room?
11. Is your street beautiful?
12. Where is the post office? library?
13. Is the post office open now? bank? library?
14. Are you busy in the morning?
15. What is your favorite animal?
16. Are you afraid of rats? spiders? snakes?

fruit

horse   lion

rat   spider

snake

VOCABULARY

afraid	dental floss	get up (v.)	more	snake
animal			mouth	spider
aspirin	forget	horse	**mouth wash**	
	front		move (v.)	teeth
bill	fruit	lion		
busy			pain	use (v.)
			rat	

EXPRESSIONS

Oh, my!	It's good for pain.	Aaay!
I'm busy.	You're in good hands.	Huh?
Don't be afraid.	at the front desk	Bye.

TEST

1. _This_ books are expensive.
   - a. This
   - b. Them
   - c. Those
   - d. They

2. Where are the glasses?
   They are on the shelf.
   - a. They
   - b. They're
   - c. There
   - d. These

3. This is Miss Jones.
   She is a secretary.
   - a. It
   - b. He
   - c. Her
   - d. She

4. _Where_ is Nick? He's at the garage.
   - a. Where
   - b. What
   - c. Who
   - d. How

5. _How_ is that woman?
   She's Nancy Paine.
   - a. Where
   - b. Who
   - c. What
   - d. How

6. What color is your car? It's _Red_ .
   - a. big
   - b. new
   - c. expensive
   - d. red

7. Mr. Bascomb isn't poor. He's _Rich_ .
   - a. happy
   - b. tall
   - c. rich
   - d. good

8. Those shoes aren't old.
   They're _Cheap_ .
   - a. new
   - b. young
   - c. big
   - d. cheap

9. Those are my post cards.
   Don't take _it_ .
   - a. it
   - b. that
   - c. they
   - d. them

10. There's Maria. Let's talk with _her_ .
    - a. him
    - b. she
    - c. her
    - d. them

11. Call Mr. Poole. Give _He_ the information.
    - a. he
    - b. him
    - c. her
    - d. it

12. The telephone is _in_ the living room.
    - a. in
    - b. on
    - c. to
    - d. at

13. The girls are _at_ the bus stop.
    - a. in
    - b. on
    - c. to
    - d. at

14. Those men are tourists.
    They're _From_ England.
    - a. of
    - b. from
    - c. for
    - d. with

15. California is a beautiful _State_ .
    - a. street
    - b. city
    - c. state
    - d. country

16. My _Address_ is 205 Oak Street.
    - a. address
    - b. telephone number
    - c. office
    - d. business

17. How much are those magazines?
    - a. They're on the table.
    - b. There are five of them.
    - c. They're two dollars each. ✓
    - d. They're three years old.

18. How old is that clock?
    - a. It's twenty years old. ✓
    - b. It's two o'clock.
    - c. It's two hundred dollars.
    - d. It's expensive.

19. Aspirin is good for _teeth_ .
    - a. work
    - b. pain
    - c. teeth
    - d. dinner

20. New York is a _____ city.
    - a. small
    - b. English
    - c. cheap
    - d. modern

CHAPTER FIVE

Present continuous

Wh- questions

a   *It's Monday morning. Mr. and Mrs. Bascomb are getting up.*

He's wearing pajamas.

She's wearing a nightgown.

He's brushing his teeth.

_____ her hair.

He's taking a shower.

_____ a bath.

He's making coffee.

_____ tea.

He's putting milk in his coffee. _____ her tea.

He's reading a magazine. _____ the newspaper.

He's eating an egg. _____ an orange.

He's kissing his wife. _____ her husband.

b

Peter and Maria are sitting
in a snack bar.

Barbara and Tino are sitting
in a coffee shop.

They're watching a football game.

_____

They're drinking Coke.

_____

They're talking to Otis.

_____

They're playing darts.

_____

They're looking at the clock.

_____

They're paying the cashier.

_____

They're saying "goodbye" to Otis.

_____

c *Ask and answer questions about the pictures.*

1. A: Where's Mr. Bascomb?
   B: He's in the bathroom.

   A: What's he doing?
   B: He's taking a shower.

2. A: Where are Barbara and Tino?
   B: They're at Mom's Cafe.

   A: What are they doing?
   B: They're drinking coffee.

3. _____ Anne?

   _____ doing?

4. _____ Fred and Barney?

   _____doing?

5. _____ Jimmy and Linda?

   _____ doing?

6. _____ Mrs. Bascomb?

   _____ doing?

7. _____ Nick?

   _____ doing?

8. _____ Otis and Gloria?

   _____ doing?

a

b

a It's Saturday night at the Student Club. Jimmy and Linda are dancing and Tony's watching them. Albert's standing by the table. He's eating a sandwich. Bill and Jane are talking to each other and Karen's walking to the door. It's eleven o'clock and she's going home.

1. What night is it?
2. What are Jimmy and Linda doing? (b)
3. What's Tony doing? (a)
4. Where's Albert standing? (c)
5. What's he eating?
6. What are Bill and Jane doing? (d)
7. What's Karen doing? (e)
8. Where's she going?

b Sam and Mabel Brown are in a small restaurant. They're sitting at a table in the corner. Sam's calling the waiter and Mabel's looking at the menu. The waiter's standing at the counter. He's reading a newspaper.

1. Where are Sam and Mabel?
2. Are they standing or sitting?
3. Who's Sam calling?
4. What's Mabel looking at?
5. Where's the waiter?
6. What's he doing?

AFFIRMATIVE

Karen's walking to the door.
She's _____ .
John's_____ .
He's _____ .

We're reading the newspaper.
They're_____ .
You're _____ .
I'm _____ .

c *Answer the following questions as indicated.*

Example: Is Albert eating an apple? (a sandwich)
    No, he's eating a sandwich.

1. Is Linda dancing with Albert? (with Jimmy)
2. Is Tony watching Karen? (Jimmy and Linda)
3. Is Karen walking to the table? (to the door)
4. Is she going to a movie? (home)
5. Is she wearing a long dress? (a short dress)

1. Are Sam and Mabel sitting in a coffee shop? (in a restaurant)
2. Is Mabel looking at Sam? (at the menu)
3. Is Sam calling the cashier? (the waiter)
4. Is the waiter standing by the table? (by the counter)
5. Is he reading a magazine? (a newspaper)

ALBERT: Hi, Jimmy. Where's your sister?

JIMMY: At home. She's helping my mother.

ALBERT: Is she washing the dishes?

JIMMY: No, she isn't.

ALBERT: What's she doing?

JIMMY: She's cleaning the windows.

ALBERT: Is your father home?

JIMMY: Yes. He's cutting the grass.

ALBERT: Why aren't you working, too?

JIMMY: It's Sunday. I'm resting today.

INTERROGATIVE

Is Linda washing the dishes ?	Are Albert and Jimmy working now ?
__ she _____ ?	__ your friends _____ ?
__ Mr. Brown _____ ?	__ they _____ ?
__ he _____ ?	__ you _____ ?

d   *Make questions as indicated.*

Examples: Linda is helping her mother.   (cleaning the windows)
         Is she cleaning the windows?

         Mr. and Mrs. Brown are at home.   (watching television)
         Are they watching television?

1. Mr. and Mrs. Bascomb are in the kitchen.   (washing the dishes)
2. Mrs. Bascomb is sitting down.   (reading a book)
3. She's having breakfast.   (eating an egg)
4. Mr. Bascomb is standing up.   (looking at his watch)
5. He's leaving the room.   (saying "goodbye")

1. Barbara and Tino are in a coffee shop.   (calling the waiter)
2. The waiter is coming.   (bringing the menu)
3. They're ordering breakfast.   (asking for coffee and eggs)
4. Barbara is very pretty today.   (wearing a new dress)
5. She's brushing her hair.   (looking in the mirror)

NEGATIVE

Linda isn't washing the dishes.	Albert and Jimmy aren't working now.
She _____.	Your friends _____.
Mr. Brown _____.	They_____.
He _____.	You _____.

e   *Make negative sentences as indicated.*

Examples: Albert and Jimmy are talking about Linda.   (Karen)
         They aren't talking about Karen.

         Mr. Brown is listening to the radio.   (his wife)
         He isn't listening to his wife.

1. Mr. and Mrs. Bascomb are having breakfast.   (dinner)
2. Mrs. Bascomb is reading a newspaper.   (a book)
3. She's eating an orange.   (an egg)
4. Mr. Bascomb is looking at his watch.   (his wife)
5. He's saying "goodbye."   ("hello")

1. Barbara and Tino are calling the waiter.   (the cashier)
2. The waiter is bringing the menu.   (the bill)
3. They're asking for coffee and eggs.   (tea and sandwiches)
4. Barbara is wearing a new dress.   (an old dress)
5. She's brushing her hair.   (her teeth)

The Brown family is in the park. It's a beautiful Sunday and the sun is shining. Mr. Brown is smoking a pipe and reading a book. Mrs. Brown is preparing lunch. She's making sandwiches and lemonade. Linda is sitting by a tree drawing pictures. Jimmy is playing football. An old man is sitting on the hill watching the game. He's smiling and thinking about the past.

a *Answer the following questions about the story.*

1. Where is the Brown family?
2. What day of the week is it?
3. Is Mr. Brown reading a magazine?
4. Is he smoking a pipe or a cigar?
5. Is Mrs. Brown preparing breakfast?
6. What's she making?
7. Where's Linda sitting?
8. What's she doing?
9. Is Jimmy playing basketball?
10. What is the old man doing?

b *Make sentences with these words.*

Examples: We/clean/kitchen
      We're cleaning the kitchen.

Anne/help/us
Anne's helping us.

1. Mrs. Golo/eat/apple
2. Mr. Golo/make/sandwich
3. They/drink/coffee
4. They/wash/dishes
5. Tino/write/letter
6. He/listen/radio
7. Barbara/brush/teeth
8. She/wear/pajamas
9. I/read/magazine
10. You/play/guitar

c *Change the following sentences to the negative.*

Examples: She's calling the hospital.
      She isn't calling the hospital.

We're going to the park.
We aren't going to the park.

1. He's buying a house.
2. She's working at the library.
3. They're going to a party.
4. They're waiting for Nancy.
5. She's writing a letter.
6. You're listening to the radio.
7. They're watching television.
8. She's preparing dinner.
9. He's reading a book.
10. We're playing cards.

d *Make questions as indicated.*

Examples: Mr. Brown is at home. (watch/television)
      Is he watching television?

Jimmy is in the bathroom. (take/shower)
Is he taking a shower?

1. Mrs. Brown is in the kitchen. (make/tea)
2. Linda is in her room. (read/book)
3. Albert is in the park. (play/football)
4. Barney is in a restaurant. (eat/dinner)
5. Nancy is at home. (write/letter)
6. Mr. Bascomb is in his office. (smoke/cigar)
7. Barbara is at a party. (wear/red dress)
8. Fred is at the snack bar. (drink/coffee)
9. Maria is at the antique shop. (buy/vase)
10. Peter is in his car. (listen to/radio)

e *Make questions with **who**, **what**, or **where**, as indicated.*

Examples: Albert's going <u>to the movies</u>.   The children are playing <u>in the park</u>.
     Where's he going?   **Where are they playing?**

         He's talking to <u>Linda</u>.   They're looking at <u>the birds</u>.
     Who's he talking to?   **What are they looking at?**

1. Barney's reading <u>a magazine</u>.   6. They're eating <u>sandwiches</u>.
2. He's waiting for <u>Nancy.</u>   7. Mrs. Brown's watching <u>television.</u>
3. He's sitting in <u>a coffee shop.</u>   8. She's sitting <u>in the living room.</u>
4. Maria's talking to <u>Peter.</u>   9. She's calling <u>Mr. Brown.</u>
5. They're standing <u>at the bus stop.</u>

f *Answer the following questions using object pronouns.*

Example: Is Peter asking <u>the waiter</u> for a glass of water?   (a menu)
     No, he's asking <u>him</u> for a menu.

1. Is Tino taking <u>Barbara</u> a magazine?   (a book)
2. Is Mrs. Brown giving <u>the children</u> a cat?   (a dog)
3. Is Linda asking <u>her father</u> for a clock?   (a watch)
4. Is Albert writing <u>Linda</u> a letter?   (a postcard)
5. Is Otis bringing <u>the boys</u> a football?   (a basketball)
6. Is Maria giving <u>Peter</u> an apple?   (a pear)
7. Is Jimmy bringing <u>his mother</u> a glass?   (a cup)
8. Is Anne taking <u>Mr. Bascomb</u> a letter?   (a telegram)
9. Is Mrs. Golo giving <u>the students</u> a dictionary?   (an encyclopedia)

a telegram

an encyclopedia

g *Complete the following sentences with suitable prepositions.*

Example: Mr. Brown is sitting ___*in*___ the living room.

1. He's writing a letter _____ his brother _____ New York.

2. Barbara's going _____ the movies _____ Tino.

3. Albert's standing _____ the bus stop.

4. He's thinking _____ Linda.

5. She's walking _____ the library _____ Jimmy.

6. Barney's having lunch _____ Nancy _____ a Mexican restaurant.

7. They're sitting _____ a table _____ the corner.

8. Barney's talking _____ the waiter _____ football.

9. Nancy's drinking a cup _____ coffee.

VOCABULARY

about	coffee shop	get	menu	policeman	tea
antique shop	Coke	goodbye	milk	prepare	teeth
	counter	grass	mirror		telegram
basketball	cut (v.)	green	Monday	radio	television
bath			mother	rest (v.)	think
bathroom	darts	hair		restaurant	today
beach	draw	help	night		
bill	drink (v.)	husband	nightgown	say	walk (v.)
breakfast				shine	water
brother	encyclopedia	kiss	pajamas	shower	wear
brush (v.)			park	sister	week
buy	family	lemonade	party	smile (v.)	wife
	football	long	pay	smoke (v.)	
cashier	for	lunch	picture	snack bar	
cigar			pipe	sun	
clean (v.)	game	make	play (v.)	Sunday	

PRONUNCIATION

	i			iy	
give	dish	big	we	beach	meet
him	with	kiss	tea	cheap	please
this	it	sit	street	eat	read
little	rich	kitchen	clean	leave	green

Give Nick this picture.
His little sister is in the kitchen.

Please meet the teacher at the museum.
The streets are clean and the tea is green.

Jimmy is cleaning the windows.
He isn't reading his magazine.

PRESENT CONTINUOUS Affirmative

He She It	's (is)	
I	'm (am)	watching television.
You We They	're (are)	

Negative

He She It	isn't (is not) 's not	
I	'm not (am not)	watching television.
You We They	aren't (are not) 're not	

Interrogative

Is	he she it	
Am	I	watching television?
Are	you we they	

Short Answers

Yes,	he she it	is.
	I	am.
	you we they	are.

No,	he she it	isn't.
	I	'm not.
	you we they	aren't.

Question with
WHAT, WHO, WHERE

Albert is eating a sandwich.	What 's (is) he eating?	A sandwich.
Linda is dancing with Jimmy.	Who 's (is) she dancing with?	Jimmy.
Sam is going to the garage.	Where 's (is) he going?	To the garage.

CHAPTER SIX

"To have"
Possessive
adjectives

Possessive of nouns
"Whose . . .?"

MRS. GOLO: You have a nice husband, Mabel.

MRS. BROWN: Yes, and he has a good wife.

MRS. GOLO: You have beautiful children.

MRS. BROWN: Yes, and they have a good mother.

MRS. GOLO: You have a wonderful family.

MRS. BROWN: That's right. We have everything.

MRS. GOLO: No, Mabel. There's one thing
                 you don't have.

MRS. BROWN: What's that?

MRS. GOLO: Humility!

AFFIRMATIVE

You have a nice family.   Peter has a good job.
They_____.   He _____.
We _____.   Maria_____.
I _____.   She_____.

a *Complete the following sentences with **have** or **has**.*

Examples: Barney *has* a red taxi.

Mr. and Mrs. Brown *have* a large refrigerator.

1. They _____ a friend named Jack.

2. He _____ two brothers.

3. You _____ a nice family.

4. Tino _____ a girlfriend named Barbara.

5. She _____ a job at the bank.

6. We _____ a good library.

7. I _____ a new radio.

8. Mrs. Bascomb _____ an intelligent husband.

9. He _____ an important job.

10. They _____ an expensive car.

a refrigerator

a radio

b *Ask and answer questions as indicated.*

Example: a brother
Student A: **Do you have a brother?**
Student B: **Yes, I do.** OR **No, I don't.**

1. a sister	6. a guitar
2. a clock	7. a record player
3. a watch	8. a camera
4. a cat	9. a football
5. a dog	10. a bicycle

a record player

a camera

ANNE: Barbara, give me your pen, please.

BARBARA: I don't have a pen. Here's a pencil.

ANNE: Thank you. Do you have a piece of paper?

BARBARA: Here you are. Is it for a letter?

ANNE: That's right. Do you have an envelope?

BARBARA: Yes. But I don't have stamps.

ANNE: That's O.K. I have stamps.

BARBARA: Oh, really? That's good.

INTERROGATIVE

Do you have an envelope ?
__ they_____ ?
__ we _____ ?
__ the girls _____ ?

Does Anne have a pen ?
____ she_____ ?
____ John _____ ?
____ he _____ ?

c   *Complete these questions.*

Examples: ____*Do*____ they have a typewriter?

____*Does*____ Albert have a telephone?

    a typewriter   a telephone

1. _____ we have a dictionary?

2. _____ she have a bicycle?

3. _____ you have a sister?

4. _____ I have your address?

5. _____ Nick have a garage?

6. _____ you have a guitar?

7. _____ Maria have a brown hat?

8. _____ they have an apartment?

9. _____ he have a lamp?

NEGATIVE

We don't have a clock.
They_____ .
You _____ .
I _____ .

Linda doesn't have a car.
Jimmy _____ .
He _____ .
Mrs. Golo _____ .

d   *Make negative sentences as indicated.*

Examples: They have a guitar. (a piano)
       But they don't have a piano.

        Mrs. Golo has a radio. (a television)
       But she doesn't have a television.

    a piano

1. We have a library. (a museum)
2. Barbara has a pencil. (a pen)
3. I have a sister. (a brother)
4. She has a hat. (an umbrella)
5. Jimmy has a football. (a basketball)
6. We have a table. (a desk)
7. She has a dog. (a cat)
8. They have an office. (a telephone)
9. He has a job. (a car)

a television (TV)

e   *Look at the pictures and answer the following questions.*

1.

Does Tino have
a wallet?

Yes, he does.

2.

Does Mrs. Bascomb
have a wallet?

No, she doesn't.
She has a handbag.

3.

Does Maria have
a bottle?

4.

Does Barbara have
a typewriter?

5.

Does Albert have
an apple?

6.

Does Simon have
a rabbit?

7.

Does Mrs. Golo
have an umbrella?

8.

Does Barney have
a truck?

9.

Does Anne have
a guitar?

f   *Look at the picture and answer the following questions.*

Examples: Do Mr. and Mrs. Wankie have a house?
           No, they don't. (They have an apartment.)

           Do they have a telephone?
           Yes, they do.

1. Do they have a record player?
2. Do they have a piano?
3. Do they have a clock?
4. Do they have a bookcase?
5. Do they have a typewriter?
6. Do they have a camera?
7. Do they have a television?
8. Do they have a dog?
9. Do they have a cat?

1.

2.

3.

4.

5.

6.

POSSESSIVE
ADJECTIVES

I have a book.	It's my book.
You have a book.	It's your book.
He has a book.	It's his book.
She has a book.	It's her book.
We have a book.	It's our book.
They have a book.	It's their book.

a   *Complete the following sentences with* **my, your, his, her, our,** *or* **their.**

Example: Peter has a clock in ____*his*____ apartment.

1. Maria has a piano in _____ apartment.

2. Mr. and Mrs. Brown have a television in _____ living room.

3. I have an umbrella in _____ car.

4. We have a good library in _____ city.

5. She has a radio in _____ room.

6. You have a beautiful vase in _____ kitchen.

7. I have a pen in _____ pocket.

8. He has a newspaper in _____ desk.

b   *Complete the following sentences.*

Example: They're painting ____*their*____ house.

1. I'm waiting for _____ sister.

2. She's talking with _____ friends.

3. They're doing _____ homework.

4. Is Jimmy helping _____ mother?

5. Linda is talking with _____ father.

6. He's cleaning _____ shoes.

7. Are you thinking about _____ family?

8. We're thinking about _____ friends.

JIMMY:	Whose car is that?
ALBERT:	It's Mr. Smith's car.
JIMMY:	It's beautiful, isn't it?
ALBERT:	It sure is.

c   *Answer the following questions as indicated.*

Examples: Whose car is that? (Mr. Smith)   Whose pens are these?   (Nancy)
     It's Mr. Smith's car.   **They're Nancy's pens.**

1. Whose watch is this? (Linda)
2. Whose lamp is that? (Mr. Bascomb)
3. Whose envelopes are those? (Barbara)
4. Whose magazines are these? (Tino)
5. Whose ball is this? (the dog)
6. Whose glasses are these? (Mrs. Golo)

d   *Answer the following questions as indicated.*

Examples: Whose bicycles are those? (the girls)   Whose house is that? (the Browns)
     They're the girls' bicycles.   **It's the Browns' house.**

1. Whose football is this?   (the boys)
2. Whose books are these?   (the students)
3. Whose car is that?   (the Golos)
4. Whose offices are those?   (the doctors)
5. Whose letters are these?   (the girls)
6. Whose apartment is that?   (the Wilsons)

e *Look at the pictures and complete the following sentences as indicated.*

Mr. Brown is a family man. He has a wife, Mabel, and two children. Their names are Jimmy and Linda. The Browns have a small house with a red roof. Their house is near the library. Mr. Brown has a Volkswagen and his wife also has a Volkswagen. His car is orange and her car is white. Right now, Mr. Brown is washing his car. Mrs. Brown is working in the garden. She's planting vegetables. Linda is helping her mother in the garden. Jimmy isn't home. He's playing football with his friends.

a *Answer the following questions about the story.*

    1. Does Mr. Brown have children?
    2. What are their names?
    3. Do the Browns have a large house with a white roof?
    4. Where is their house?
    5. What kind of car does Mr. Brown have?
    6. What color is his car?
    7. What color is Mrs. Brown's car?
    8. Do the Browns have a garden?
    9. What's Mr. Brown doing now?
  10. What's Mrs. Brown doing?
  11. What's Linda doing?
  12. Is Jimmy helping, too?

b *Answer the following questions using short answers.*

    Examples: Does Tino have a girlfriend named Maria?
           No, he doesn't.

             Does he have a girlfriend named Barbara?
             Yes, he does.

    1. Does Sam Brown have a white hat?
    2. Does he have a big car?
    3. Does Jimmy have a sister named Linda?
    4. Does she have blond hair?
    5. Does Barbara have blond hair?
    6. Does Nick have a restaurant?
    7. Does he have a garage?
    8. Does Barney have a taxi?
    9. Does Maria have a taxi?

c *Make questions as indicated.*

    Examples: Mr. and Mrs. Golo don't have a daughter. (a son)
           Do they have a son?

             Otis doesn't have a radio. (a television)
             Does he have a television?

    1. They don't have a desk. (a table)
    2. Barbara doesn't have a pen. (a pencil)
    3. We don't have a French dictionary. (a Spanish dictionary)
    4. He doesn't have a hat. (a coat)
    5. They don't have a cat. (a dog)
    6. Barney doesn't have a clock. (a watch)
    7. He doesn't have a wife. (a girlfriend)
    8. They don't have a house. (an apartment)
    9. She doesn't have a piano. (a guitar)

d *Answer the following questions in the negative as indicated.*

Examples: Where's Barbara's car?   Where's the Browns' apartment?
           She doesn't have a car.   **They don't have an apartment.**

1. Where's their truck?   6. Where's their football?
2. Where's Sam's dictionary?   7. Where's Albert's bicycle?
3. Where's Mrs. Golo's umbrella?   8. Where's his guitar?
4. Where's her hat?   9. Where's your dog?
5. Where's the children's desk?

e *Change the following sentences using the possive adjective.*

Example: You have an interesting job. _Your job is interesting._

1. We have a wonderful library. _____

2. I have a new camera. _____

3. She has an Italian boyfriend. _____

4. They have expensive dictionaries. _____

5. You have an intelligent sister. _____

6. Mrs. Brown has a wonderful family. _____

7. Albert has a black umbrella. _____

8. We have a small apartment. _____

9. You have a beautiful garden. _____

f *Make questions as indicated.*

Examples: Look at that car.   Look at those bicycles.
           Whose car is it?   **Whose bicycles are they?**

1. Look at that gun.   4. Look at those flowers.   7. Look at this dress.
2. Look at this hat.   5. Look at that dog.   8. Look at that camera.
3. Look at these stamps.   6. Look at these books.   9. Look at those pictures.

g *Answer the following questions about yourself.*

1. What nationality are you?   6. What do you have in your pocket? wallet? handbag?
2. What city are you from?   7. Do you have a typewriter? a radio? a telephone?
3. What time is it?   8. What's your address?
4. What are you doing now?   9. Is your house near the post office?
5. Where's your dictionary?   10. What street is the post office on?

VOCABULARY

also	garden	kind	piece	their
apartment	girlfriend		pocket	thing
		name (v.)		TV
boyfriend	handbag		really	typewriter
brown	have	O.K.	record player	
but	homework	our	refrigerator	vegetable
	humility		roof	
camera		paint (v.)		wallet
	important	paper	son	white
daughter	interesting	pen	stamp (n.)	whose
		pencil		wonderful
everything	job	piano	taxi	

EXPRESSIONS

What kind is it?   Oh, really?   That's good.   of course   right now
It sure is.

PRONUNCIATION

	ae			**e**	
happy	class	ask	red	telephone	ready
sad	handbag	man	desk	expensive	envelope
glad	stand	candle	bed	dress	television
bad	lamp	camera	pen	letter	message

Nancy has a black hat.   The red dress is very expensive.
The happy dancer is laughing at the fat cat.   Fred's letter is in the envelope.

Ellen has a telegram in her handbag.
The black hat is next to the red lamp.

TO HAVE   Affirmative

He She	has	
I You We They	have	a car.

Negative

He She	doesn't (does not)	
I You We They	don't (do not)	have a car.

Interrogative

Does	he she	
Do	I you we they	have a car?

Short Answers

Yes,	he she	does.
	I you we they	do.

No,	he she	doesn't.
	I you we they	don't.

POSSESSIVE ADJECTIVES

It's	my your our their his her	house.

Questions with WHOSE

Whose	radio is this? pens are these?

Whose	house is that? bicycles are those?

POSSESSIVE OF NOUNS

It's Mrs. Golo's radio.
They're Linda's pens.

It's the Browns' house.
They're the girls' bicycles.

CHAPTER SEVEN

"There is"/
"there are"
Uncountables

"To want" and
"to like"
Possessive
pronouns

a   There's a dog under the table.
_____ chair by the table.
_____ typewriter on the table.
_____ lamp behind the typewriter.
_____ vase next to the typewriter.
_____ rose in the vase.
_____ cup in front of the vase.

b   There are some cars in the street.
_____ people at the bus stop.
_____ birds on the sidewalk.
_____ bicycles under the tree.
_____ children in front of the theater.
_____ tables and chairs on the sidewalk.

c   *Answer the following questions, using short answers.*

Examples: Is there a typewriter on the table?   Is there a book on the table?
          Yes, there is.   **No, there isn't.**

1. Is there a cup on the table?
2. Is there a glass on the table?
3. Is there a bottle on the table?
4. Is there a vase on the table?
5. Is there a rose in the vase?
6. Is there a chair by the table?
7. Is there a magazine on the chair?
8. Is there a dog under the table?
9. Is there a cat under the table?

d   *Answer the following questions as indicated.*

Examples: Are there any cars in the street?   Are there any buses in the street?
          Yes, there are.   **No, there aren't.**

1. Are there any trucks in the street?
2. Are there any people at the bus stop?
3. Are there any people at Joe's Cafe?
4. Are there any birds on the sidewalk?
5. Are there any birds in the tree?
6. Are there any bicycles under the tree?
7. Are there any tables and chairs on the sidewalk?
8. Are there any glasses on the tables?
9. Are there any children in front of the theater?

e   *Answer the following questions.*

Example: How many cars are there in the street?
         There are three cars in the street.

1. How many people are there at the bus stop?
2. How many birds are there on the sidewalk?
3. How many bicycles are there under the tree?
4. How many chairs are there on the sidewalk?
5. How many tables are there on the sidewalk?
6. How many children are there in front of the theater?

1. How many days are there in a week?
2. How many months are there in a year?
3. How many hours are there in a day?
4. How many minutes are there in an hour?
5. How many people are there in your family?
6. How many pages are there in this book?

f   *Complete the following sentences about the picture.*

1. There's a bus in the street. It's a school bus.
2. _____ garden in the front yard. _____ vegetable garden.
3. _____ fence around the garden. _____ wire fence.
4. _____ table near the garden. _____ picnic table.

1. There are some cans on the sidewalk. They're trash cans.
2. _____ trees next to the house. _____ peach trees.
3. _____ bottles on the table. _____ milk bottles.
4. _____ boots on the steps. _____ cowboy boots.

g   *Answer the following questions about the picture.*

Examples: What is there in the street?   What is there on the sidewalk?
            There's a bus in the street.   **There are some cans on the sidewalk.**

            What kind of bus is it?   What kind of cans are they?
            It's a school bus.   **They're trash cans.**

1. What is there next to the house?   4. What is there near the garden?
    What kind of trees are they?   What kind of table is it?
2. What is there in the front yard?   5. What is there on the table?
    What kind of garden is it?   What kind of bottles are they?
3. What is there around the garden?   6. What is there on the steps?
    What kind of fence is it?   What kind of boots are they?

UNCOUNTABLES

There's some bread on the table.
_____ cheese _____.
_____ butter _____.
_____ milk _____.

h *Ask and answer questions about the pictures, as in the example.*

1.

a bottle of milk

STUDENT A:

What's in the bottle?

STUDENT B:

There's some milk in the bottle.

2.

a pitcher of lemonade

3.

a bowl of soup

4.

a box of cereal

5.

a jar of mustard

6.

a cup of coffee

7.

a dish of ice cream

8.

a can of tomato juice

i   *Complete the following sentences with **there's a**, **there's some**, or **there are some**.*

Examples: ___*There's a*___ plate on the table.

          ___*There are some*___ cookies on the plate.

1. _____ coffeepot on the table.

   _____ coffee in the coffeepot.

2. _____ bread on the table.

   _____ knives next to the bread.

3. _____ bottle on the table.

   _____ milk in the bottle.

4. _____ sandwiches on the table.

   _____ cheese next to the sandwiches.

5. _____ dish on the table.

   _____ cherries in the dish.

WAITRESS: What do you want for lunch, sir?

PETER SMITH: I want some coffee and a ham sandwich.

WAITRESS: Do you want mayonnaise on your sandwich?

PETER SMITH: No, thank you. I don't like mayonnaise.

WAITRESS: Do you like mustard?

PETER SMITH: Yes, I do. And give me some ketchup, please.

WAITRESS: Yes, sir. Here's a bottle of ketchup.

PETER SMITH: Thank you very much.

AFFIRMATIVE

Peter likes ketchup.   They like lemonade.
He _____ .   We _____ .
Maria _____ .   You _____ .
She _____ .   I _____ .

a   *Make sentences as indicated.*

Example: Peter likes ketchup.   (a bottle of ketchup)
   He wants a bottle of ketchup.

1. He likes coffee.   (a cup of coffee)
2. Linda likes milk.   (a glass of milk)
3. She likes ice cream.   (a dish of ice cream)
4. Tino likes tomato juice.   (a can of tomato juice)

Example: I like cake.   (a piece of cake)
   I want a piece of cake.

a piece of cake   a slice of bread

1. They like wine.   (a bottle of wine)
2. I like bread.   (a slice of bread)
3. We like soup.   (a bowl of soup)
4. They like French fries.   (a plate of French fries)

a plate of
French fries
(fried potatoes)

NEGATIVE

Peter doesn't like mayonnaise.   They don't like Coke.
He _____ .   We _____ .
Maria _____ .   You _____ .
She _____ .   I _____ .

b   *Make the following sentences negative.*

Examples: Peter likes mustard.   (mayonnaise)
   But he doesn't like mayonnaise.

   Mr. and Mrs. Bascomb like French food.   (English food)
   But they don't like English food.

1. They like New York.   (Chicago)
2. He likes opera.   (ballet)
3. She likes Mr. Poole.   (his wife)
4. Barbara and Tino like tomato juice.   (tomato soup)
5. He likes coffee.   (tea)
6. She likes spaghetti.   (pizza)
7. We like oranges.   (pears)
8. Albert likes chocolate ice cream.   (chocolate cake)
9. I like tomatoes.   (potatoes)

POSSESSIVE ADJECTIVES	POSSESSIVE PRONOUNS
my	mine
your	yours
his	his
her	hers
our	ours
their	theirs

c   *Make sentences with* **mine, yours, his, hers, ours,** *or* **theirs,** *as indicated.*

Examples: This is your book. *This book is yours.*

These are their typewriters. *These typewriters are theirs.*

1. This is my hat. _____

2. That's his radio. _____

3. These are our magazines. _____

4. This is her handbag. _____

5. That's their camera. _____

6. This is my dog and that's her dog. _____

7. This is our desk. _____

8. Those are your pens. _____

9. These are her post cards. _____

d   *Answer in the negative.*

Examples: Is this your umbrella?   Are those his pictures?
           No, it isn't mine.   **No, they aren't his.**

1. Is this his radio?   6. Is that his chair?
2. Is that her dictionary?   7. Is that their apartment?
3. Is that your car?   8. Is this our typewriter?
4. Are those our coats?   9. Are these your stamps?
5. Are these her pencils?

There's an old white house on Bunker Hill. It's a traditional American house.
It has large windows and a wide green door. There's a statue of a woman in
front of the house. And there are red roses in the garden. The trees behind
the house are tall and very beautiful. The house belongs to an old professor.
He's a butterfly expert. His name is Dr. Pasto. The people of Bunker Hill like
him. He's very friendly. He has visitors every day. At the moment, Dr. Pasto
is chasing butterflies. He wants them for his collection.

a *Answer the following questions.*

1. What's on Bunker Hill?
2. What kind of house is it?
3. What color is the door?
4. Is there a statue of a man in front of the house?
5. What's in the garden?

6. Where are the trees?
7. What are they like?
8. Who does the house belong to?
9. Do the people of Bunker Hill like him?
10. What's Dr. Pasto doing now?
11. Why does he want butterflies?

b *Look at the picture above and answer the following questions.*

Examples: What's in the bathroom? (a mirror)
There's a mirror in the bathroom.

What's in the bedroom? (some flowers)
There are some flowers in the bedroom.

1. What's in the kitchen? (a stove)
                                   (some pots)
                                   (a sink)
2. What's in the living room? (some chairs)
                                        (a table)
                                        (a television)
3. What's in the bathroom? (a bathtub)
                                     (a toilet)
                                     (a wash basin)
4. What's in the bedroom? (a bed)
                                    (some flowers)
                                    (a picture)

c   *You are in a restaurant.   Student A (waiter/waitress) asks Student B (customer) what he/she wants for lunch.   The customer chooses from the following:*

coffee	ham sandwich	mayonnaise
milk	cheese sandwich	mustard
orange juice	hamburger	ketchup
lemonade	hot dog	

Student A: What do you want for lunch, _____ ?

Student B: I want some _____ and a _____ .

Student A: Do you want _____ on your _____ ?

Student B: Yes, please.

　　　　　　OR   No, thank you.   I don't like _____ .

d   *Make questions as indicated.*

Examples: Nick and Barney don't like basketball. (football)
　　　　　　Do they like football?

　　　　　　Barbara doesn't have a car. (a bicycle)
　　　　　　Does she have a bicycle?

1. My sister doesn't like apple juice. (orange juice)
2. Jimmy and Linda don't have a cat. (a dog)
3. They don't want a new television. (a new radio)
4. Dr. Pasto doesn't have a stamp collection. (a butterfly collection)
5. Maria doesn't like red roses. (yellow roses)
6. Albert doesn't want cake. (ice cream)
7. Mr. and Mrs. Bascomb don't like rock music. (classical music)
8. Anne doesn't have a job at the library. (a job at the bank)
9. She doesn't want a new hat. (a new dress)

e   *Answer the following questions about yourself.*

1. Are you thirsty?
2. Do you want a glass of water?
3. Are you hungry?
4. Do you want a sandwich?
5. Do you like ice cream? cake?
6. Do you like lemonade? coffee?
7. What's your favorite food? drink?
8. What's your favorite sport?
9. Do you like football? basketball? baseball?
10. Is baseball popular in your country?
11. Who is your favorite athlete?
12. What's your favorite team?

a baseball
game

f   *Make a negative sentence for each picture using the verb **to like**.*

1. Peter *doesn't like mayonnaise* .

2. Barbara and Tino *don't like flies* .

3. Mrs. Golo _____ .

4. The students _____ .

5. Jack _____ .

6. Anne _____ .

7. The Bascombs _____ .

8. Dr. Pasto _____ .

g *Make sentences with **mine, yours, his, hers, ours,** or **theirs.***

Examples: This is my chair.   Those are her photographs.
           This chair is mine.   **Those photographs are hers.**

1. That's our dictionary.   6. This is our typewriter.
2. This is his notebook.   7. That's her handbag.
3. That's their table.   8. Those are my magazines.
4. Those are your stamps.   9. Those are his cards.
5. These are my envelopes.   10. This is your umbrella.

h *Complete the following sentences, using suitable prepositions.*

Example: Barbara is sitting ___*with*___ Tino ___*in*___ his car.

1. She's talking _____ her job _____ the bank.

2. Albert and Linda are sitting _____ a coffee shop.

3. She wants a bowl _____ soup _____ lunch.

4. Jimmy is buying some stamps _____ the post office _____ Maple Street.

5. He's writing a letter _____ a friend _____ Florida.

6. The post office is open _____ nine _____ five.

7. That old house belongs _____ Dr. Pasto.

8. He's working _____ the garden.

9. I'm giving this butterfly _____ Dr. Pasto _____ his collection.

a balcony

i *Answer the following questions about your house or apartment.*

1. How old is your house/apartment?
2. How many rooms are there? Are they large or small?
3. What is your living room like? How many windows are there?
4. What color are the walls? Are there any pictures on the walls?
5. Are there any plants or flowers in your home?
6. What is the kitchen like? Is it large or small? Is it next to the living room?
7. What is the furniture like? Is it comfortable?
8. Do you have a balcony? a fireplace?
9. What's the best thing about your house/apartment?

a fireplace

j *Write a short composition about your house or apartment.*

VOCABULARY

any	cereal	fried	mine	potato	toilet
around	chase	friendly	moment	professor	tomato
athlete	cheese	front	month		traditional
	cherry		music	rock music	trash
baseball	chocolate	ham	mustard	rose	
bathtub	classical	hour			visitor
bed	coffeepot		notebook	sidewalk	
bedroom	collection	ice cream		sink (n.)	waitress
belong	cookie		opera	slice (n.)	want
boot		jar		some	wash basin
bowl	Dr.	juice	page	soup	watch (v.)
box			people	spaghetti	why
bread	every	ketchup	photograph	sport	wide
butter	expert	knife	picnic	statue	wine
butterfly			pitcher	step (n.)	wire
	fence	life	pizza	stove	
cafe	flies (n.)	like (v.)	plant (v.)		yard
cake	food		plate	team	yellow
can (n.)	French fries	mayonnaise	popular	theater	

EXPRESSIONS

Thank you very much.

PRONUNCIATION

	ay			ey	
time	buy	mine	cake	vase	make
write	pipe	by	paper	bookcase	take
shine	white	slice	airplane	favorite	eight
bicycle	pilot	like	plate	chase	game

Simon's pipe is by the typewriter.
The white bicycle is behind the library.

Take the vase and the plates to Miss Paine.
Mabel is making a cake today.

I'm waiting for an airplane pilot.
Jane likes cake and ice cream.

THERE IS/THERE ARE   Affirmative

There's (There is)	a bottle	
There are	some glasses	on the table.
There's (There is)	some cake	

It's	a large bottle.
They're (They are)	small glasses.
It's	chocolate cake.

Interrogative

Is there	a bottle	
Are there	any glasses	on the table?
Is there	any cake	

Short answers

	there is.
Yes,	there are.
	there is.

	there isn't.
No,	there aren't.
	there isn't.

Question with HOW MANY

How many	bottles glasses	are there?

There's There are	one (bottle). five (glasses).

POSSESSIVE ADJECTIVES

It's	my your our their his her	house.

POSSESSIVE PRONOUNS

It's	mine. yours. ours. theirs. his. hers.

NOUNS AS MODIFIERS

It's a	school bus. business letter.
They're	apple trees. office buildings.

WANT Affirmative

He She	wants	a glass of water.
I You We They	want	

Negative

He She	doesn't (does not)	want a glass of water.
I You We They	don't (do not)	

Interrogative

Does	he she	want a glass of water?
Do	I you we they	

Short answers

Yes,	he she	does.
	I you we they	do.

No,	he she	doesn't.
	I you we they	don't.

CHAPTER EIGHT

Review

THE ART EXHIBITION

Today there's an art exhibition in City Park. Otis Jackson has some of his new paintings in the exhibition. He's showing them to the public for the first time. Otis is a very good artist. His paintings are an expression of his strong personality. He's a vegetarian; that's why Otis paints fruit and vegetables. He's also a Sagittarian; his birthday is in December. Sagittarians are intelligent people, and they like unusual things. The fruit and vegetables in Otis's paintings are different from ordinary fruit and vegetables. They're very large and have strange shapes and colors.

At the moment Otis is talking to some art lovers, including Dr. Pasto. They're standing around some of his paintings of fruit. Otis is a good talker, and he has some interesting ideas on art.

"Art is life," says Otis. "My paintings are me."

"That's certainly true," says Dr. Pasto. "You and your paintings are very original."

"Thank you, Dr. Pasto."

"This is a fine painting here, Otis. The colors are beautiful."

"You're looking at one of my favorite compositions. It's called 'The Happy Butterfly.' "

"Is it for sale, Otis?"

"Yes, sir."

"How much do you want for it?"

"I'm asking eighty dollars."

"Let's see. I think I have eighty dollars in my wallet. Yes. Here you are, Otis."

"Thank you, Dr. Pasto. You have a good painting there. Enjoy it."

   a   *Answer the following questions about the story.*

    1. Where's the art exhibition?
    2. Does Otis have his new paintings in the exhibition?
    3. Is he an ordinary artist?
    4. Docs Otis like meat?
    5. Why does he paint fruit and vegetables?
    6. Is Otis a Sagitarian?
    7. When is his birthday?
    8. What are the fruit and vegetables in Otis's paintings like?
    9. Who is Otis talking to?
   10. What does Otis say about art?
   11. What is Dr. Pasto looking at?
   12. How much does Otis want for the painting?

b *Make questions with **who**, **where**, or **what** as indicated.*

Examples: The art exhibition is <u>in City Park</u>.   Otis is talking to <u>Dr. Pasto</u>.
Where's the art exhibition?   **Who's he talking to?**

He likes <u>fruit and vegetables</u>.
What does he like?

1. Dr. Pasto has <u>a butterfly collection</u>.
2. His house is <u>on Bunker Hill</u>.
3. He's talking to <u>a friend</u>.
4. Mr. Bascomb is <u>at the antique shop</u>.
5. He wants <u>an old lamp</u>.

6. He's calling <u>the salesman</u>.
7. Maria is sitting with <u>Peter</u>.
8. They're <u>at the movies</u>.
9. They're watching <u>an Italian film</u>.

c *Answer the following questions using opposites.*

Examples: Is Peter married?   Are Mr. and Mrs. Golo fat?
No, he isn't. He's single.   **No, they aren't. They're thin.**

1. Is Mr. Bascomb poor?
2. Is his car cheap?
3. Are Jimmy and Linda old?
4. Is Barbara tall?

5. Is Albert thin?
6. Is his umbrella white?
7. Are London and Tokyo small cities?
8. Is the Volkswagen a big car?

d *Answer the following questions as indicated.*

Examples: How much is Otis's painting? (80 dollars) *It's eighty dollars* .

How old is City Park. (92 years) *It's ninety-two years old* .

1. How old is Dr. Pasto? (58 years) _____ .

2. How old is Barbara? (24 years) _____ .

3. How old is Tino? (29 years) _____ .

4. How old is the museum? (31 years) _____ .

5. How much is the antique chair? (87 dollars) _____ .

6. How much is the bicycle? (65 dollars) _____ .

7. How much are the typewriters? (96 dollars) _____ .

8. How much are the dictionaries? (9 dollars) _____ .

e *Look at page 121. Ask and answer questions about movies, TV programs, music and books.*

Student A: **What kind of movies do you like?**   **What's your favorite movie?**
Student B: **I like comedies and dramas.**   **Star Wars.**

MOVIES: musicals, comedies, westerns, science fiction, dramas.

TV PROGRAMS: dramas, news, sports, cartoons, comedies.

MUSIC: rock, jazz, disco, classical, popular.

BOOKS: mysteries, love stories, biographies, historical books.

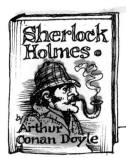   

Who is your favorite author, actor, singer, TV star?

f   *Look at the picture and answer the following questions.*

1. How many dogs are there in the street?
2. How many firemen are there on the fire truck?
3. How many children are there in front of the snack bar?
4. How many policemen are there in the street?
5. How many passengers are there in Barney's taxi?
6. How many bicycles are there in front of the movie theater?
7. How many cats are there on the roof?
8. How many birds are there in the picture?
9. How many trees are there in the picture?

g   *Answer the following questions about the picture using suitable prepositions.*

Examples: Where are the dogs? ___*They're in*___ the street.

Where's the Volkswagen? ___*It's between*___ the taxi and the bus.

1. Where's the taxi? _____ the Volkswagen.

2. Where's the bus? _____ the Volkswagen.

3. Where's Mr. Bascomb? _____ the corner.

4. Where are the firemen? _____ the fire truck.

5. Where are the Japanese tourists? _____ Barney's taxi.

6. Where are the children? _____ the snack bar.

7. Where's the snack bar? _____ the street from the drugstore.

8. Where are the bicycles? _____ the movie theater.

9. Where's the pet shop? _____ the snack bar.

10. Where's the cat? _____ the roof.

h   *Answer the following questions about the picture.*

Examples: Is Mr. Bascomb crossing the street?   Is he looking at the fire truck?
   No, he isn't. He's standing at the corner.   **Yes, he is.**

1. Is he smoking?   6. Are the children eating hot dogs?
2. Is he wearing a hat?   7. Is the old woman closing the window?
3. Is Barney driving his taxi?   8. Are the dogs chasing the policeman?
4. Does he have three passengers?   9. Are the bicycles in front of the movie theater?
5. Are they Italian?   10. Is the drugstore next to the snack bar?

i   *Answer the following questions about the picture.*

Example: Where is Mr. Bascomb standing?
   He's standing at the corner.

1. What's he looking at?   7. What are the children eating?
2. Is he smoking a pipe or a cigar?   8. What are they looking at?
3. What's Barney doing?   9. What's the old woman doing?
4. What are his passengers doing?   10. Is the young woman leaving the drugstore
5. Where's the policeman standing?   or the movie theater?
6. What are the dogs chasing?

j   *Complete the following sentences using object pronouns.*

Examples: There's Maria. Let's talk with _**her**_ .

          I'm coming. Wait for _**me**_ .

1. Call the waiter. Ask _____ for the menu.

2. We're thirsty. Please bring _____ some water.

3. This meat is no good. Don't eat _____ .

4. Those aren't your matches. Don't take _____ .

5. Here's my telephone number. Call _____ tonight.

6. We don't have the school's address. Please give _____ to _____ .

7. The students are in the classroom. Mrs. Golo is with _____ .

8. Mrs. Golo is a good teacher. The students like _____ .

9. Where's my dictionary? Do you have _____ .

10. Marty has chocolate on his face. Look at _____ .

k   *Complete the following sentences using possessive adjectives and possessive pronouns.*

Examples: Mr. and Mrs. Golo are cleaning _**their**_ house.

          Give me that magazine! It's _**mine**_.

1. Mr. Bascomb is talking to _____ secretary.

2. What does she have in _____ handbag?

3. That dictionary belongs to us. It's _____ .

4. Take this book to Jimmy and Linda. It's _____ .

5. I have _____ classes in the morning and Linda has _____ in the afternoon.

6. Albert says those matches are _____ .

7. Don't take that pen! It isn't _____ .

8. You have _____ birthday in July and I have _____ in August.

9. We're waiting for _____ friends. They're coming in _____ car.

l   *Answer the following questions in the negative.*

Examples: Is Linda drinking coffee?   Are the Browns planting tomatoes?
           No. She doesn't like coffee.   **No. They don't like tomatoes.**

1. Is Albert playing basketball?
2. Are Peter and Maria eating spaghetti?
3. Is Mr. Golo watching television?
4. Is Mrs. Golo listening to rock music?
5. Are they drinking tea?
6. Is Peter asking for mayonnaise?
7. Are Mr. and Mrs. Bascomb going to the beach?
8. Is Barney drinking milk?
9. Is Nancy eating chocolate cake?

m   *Answer the following questions about yourself.*

1. Are you a good talker?
2. What do you talk about with your friends?
3. Are you a music lover?
4. What do you think of rock music? jazz?
5. Do you have a record player at home?
6. How many records do you have?
7. What is your favorite band? song?
8. Do you have a big family?
9. How many brothers and sisters do you have? Where are they now?

VOCABULARY

actor	different	idea	ordinary	show (v.)
art	disco	include	original	song
August	drama			star
author	drive (v.)	Japanese	painting	story
		jazz	passenger	strange
band	enjoy	July	personality	strong
biography	exhibition		pet shop	
birthday	expression	love (n.)	poker	talker
		lover	popular	true
cartoon	face		program	
certainly	fireman	many	public	unusual
cigarette	fire truck	meat		
comedy	first	musical	Sagittarian	vegetarian
composition		mystery	sale	
cross (v.)	historical		science fiction	western
December	hot dog	news	shape	when

EXPRESSIONS

at the moment   for sale   Let's see.

TEST

1. This is Mr. Poole.
   _____ is a teacher.

   a. Him   c. He
   b. It   d. She

2. _____ book is interesting.

   a. These   c. Those
   b. There   d. This

3. _____ flowers are beautiful.

   a. Those   c. That
   b. There   d. This

4. The table is _____ the kitchen.

   a. on   c. to
   b. at   d. in

5. The umbrella is _____ the floor.

   a. at   c. in
   b. on   d. to

6. Nancy is _____ the airport.

   a. to   c. at
   b. on   d. with

7. Tino _____ thirsty.

   a. is   c. have
   b. has   d. are

8. Are _____ pretty girls?

   a. she   c. them
   b. they   d. her

9. The flowers _____ in the vase.

   a. are   c. be
   b. is   d. have

10. Tino isn't short. He's _____.

    a. poor   c. sad
    b. happy   d. tall

11. Those books aren't cheap.
    They're _____.

    a. old   c. small
    b. expensive   d. rich

12. They _____ the bank.

    a. are going   c. are going to
    b. is going   d. going to

13. _____ is that? It's a coffee pot.

    a. Who   c. Where
    b. How   d. What

14. _____ He's at the garage.

    a. Where is he?   c. Who is he?
    b. What is he?   d. How is he?

15. _____ They're fine, thank you.

    a. Who are they?   c. How are they?
    b. What are they?   d. Where are they?

16. _____ is she going? To the market.

    a. What   c. Who
    b. Where   d. How

17. _____ is he? He's Dr. Pasto.

    a. Where   c. How
    b. What   d. Who

18. Wait _____ Anne.

    a. for   c. to
    b. at   d. from

19. Who is she looking _____?

    a. on   c. to
    b. at   d. from

20. He's listening _____ the radio.

    a. at   c. of
    b. in   d. to

21. Talk _____ them.

    a. to   c. on
    b. at   d. of

22. Put these glasses _____ the table.

    a. to   c. on
    b. in   d. at

23. They don't have _____ books.

    a. there   c. theirs
    b. their   d. them

24. This magazine is _____.

    a. to her   c. hers
    b. her   d. of her

25. That desk is _____.

    a. mine   c. me
    b. my   d. to me

26. Whose apartment is that?
    It's _____.

    a. to him   c. his
    b. Mr. Jones   d. him

27. Give the flowers _____.

    a. them   c. to they
    b. their   d. to them

28. That man is hungry.
    Give _____ some food.

    a. he   c. his
    b. her   d. him

29. Mrs. Jones is in Italy.
    Write _____ a letter.

    a. to her   c. hers
    b. her   d. him

30. Do they have a car?
    No, they _____.

    a. don't   c. aren't
    b. doesn't   d. have

31. _____ an apple in the kitchen.

    a. It has   c. It's
    b. There are   d. There's

32. Where are the cups?
    _____ on the shelf.

    a. They're   c. There is
    b. There are   d. Their

33. What are those?
    _____ dictionaries.

    a. There are   c. They're
    b. There's some   d. It's a

34. _____ milk in the bottle.

    a. There's some   c. It's a
    b. There's a   d. There are

35. _____ letters on the desk.

    a. There's   c. Their
    b. There are   d. They're

36. What time is it? _____

    a. It's hot.   c. It's two o'clock.
    b. It's ten dollars.   d. It's six years old.

37. How old is that watch? _____

    a. It's one o'clock.   c. It's expensive.
    b. It's fifty dollars.   d. It's six years old.

38. How much is that typewriter? _____

    a. It's in the office.   c. It's six years old.
    b. It's fifty dollars.   d. It's very good.

39. Jimmy _____ ice cream.

    a. have   c. likes
    b. like   d. want

40. She's thirsty.
    She _____ a glass of water.

    a. wants   c. have
    b. want   d. likes

CHAPTER NINE

Present simple **Adverbs of frequency**

a

b

a   Barbara Sherman is a secretary
at the City Bank. She works
every day from nine to five.
She lives a long way from her job,
and she doesn't drive a car.
She always takes the bus
to work.

1. Is Barbara a teacher or a secretary?
2. What hours does she work?
3. Does she live near her job?
4. Does she drive a car?
5. How does she go to work?

b   Sam Brown lives in Wickam City.
Every morning he gets up at seven
o'clock and takes a shower. Then he
gets dressed and eats breakfast.
Sam always has bananas and apple
juice for breakfast.

1. Where does Mr. Brown live?
2. When does he get up?
3. Does he take a bath or a shower?
4. What does he do before breakfast?
5. What does he have for breakfast?

AFFIRMATIVE

Barbara works at the bank.
She_____.
Mr. Bascomb _____.
He _____.

They work every day.
You _____.
We _____.
I _____.

c   *Answer the following questions as indicated.*

Examples: Does Barbara work from nine to five?
          Yes, she works from nine to five every day.

          Do the children walk to school?
          Yes, they walk to school every day.

1. Does Peter drive to work?
2. Does Anne play the guitar?
3. Do Mr. and Mrs. Bascomb read the newspaper?
4. Does Sam eat bananas?
5. Does Mabel work in the garden?
6. Does Linda help her mother?
7. Do Barbara and Tino listen to the radio?
8. Does Tino drink coffee?
9. Does Barbara take the bus?

ANNE: Do you have a boyfriend, Barbara?

BARBARA: Yes, I do. His name's Tino.

ANNE: Tell me about him.

BARBARA: He's tall and handsome, and
            his family comes from Italy.

ANNE: Does he speak Italian?

BARBARA: Not with me. I don't understand
            a word of it.

ANNE: Does he have a good job?

BARBARA: Yes. He works for his father.

ANNE: What kind of business does his
            father have?

BARBARA: He has an Italian restaurant.

INTERROGATIVE

Does Tino speak Italian?   Do the Martinolis come from Italy?
_____ he _____?   ____ our neighbors _____?
_____ Maria _____?   ____ your friends _____?
_____ she _____?   ____ those people _____?

d   *Make questions as indicated.*

Examples: Tino speaks Italian.   (French)
          Does he speak French, too?

          Jimmy and Linda walk to school.   (home)
          Do they walk home, too?

1. Barbara works at the bank. (at home)
2. She lives a long way from her job. (a long way from her boyfriend)
3. Barney drives a taxi. (a bus)
4. Peter and Maria like Japanese food.   (Mexican food)
5. She drinks tea. (coffee)
6. He has a sports car. (a motorcycle)
7. Albert and Jimmy like hamburgers. (hot dogs)
8. They want some ketchup. (some mustard)
9. Dr. Pasto chases butterflies. (dogs)

NEGATIVE

Barbara doesn't understand Italian.   They don't work at night.
She _____.   You _____.
Mr. Bascomb _____.   We _____.
He _____.   I _____.

e   *Make negative sentences as indicated.*

Examples: Anne and Barbara don't work on Sunday. (on Saturday)
          They don't work on Saturday, either.

          Barbara doesn't live near the bank. (near the hospital)
          She doesn't live near the hospital, either.

1. Otis doesn't like meat. (chicken)
2. He doesn't eat breakfast every day. (lunch every day)
3. Mr. and Mrs. Brown don't have a big car. (a big house)
4. They don't clean the kitchen every day. (the bathroom every day)
5. Anne doesn't speak French. (Spanish)
6. She doesn't know Tino. (Barney)
7. Jimmy and Linda don't like cold weather. (hot weather)
8. They don't go to the beach every day. (to the park every day)
9. Mr. Bascomb doesn't understand Italian. (German)

Otis <u>always</u> eats
fruit and vegetables.

He <u>never</u> eats meat.

Johnny <u>often</u> goes to
the movies.

He <u>seldom</u> watches television.

Mr. Bascomb <u>usually</u>
drinks coffee.

He <u>sometimes</u> drinks tea.

ADVERBS OF FREQUENCY

They always get up at six o'clock.
_____ usually _____.
_____ often _____.
_____ sometimes _____.
_____ seldom _____.
_____ never _____.

a *Add always, usually, often, sometimes, seldom, or never to the following sentences.*

Examples: Otis eats meat. (never)
Otis never eats meat.

Mr. and Mrs. Bascomb listen to classical music. (always)
Mr. and Mrs. Bascomb always listen to classical music.

1. He drinks coffee. (usually)
2. She wears expensive clothes. (often)
3. Anne and Barbara work on Sunday. (never)
4. Barbara takes the red bus. (always)
5. Anne plays the guitar. (often)
6. Barney gets up at seven o'clock. (seldom)
7. Jimmy and Linda walk to school. (usually)
8. Albert plays football. (sometimes)
9. Nancy listens to rock music. (seldom)

INTERROGATIVE

Do they always take the bus?
_____ usually _____?
_____ often _____?
_____ ever_____?

NEGATIVE

They don't always take the bus.
_____ usually _____ .
_____ often _____ .
_____ ever _____ .

b *Add always, usually, often, or ever to the following sentences.*

Examples: Does Barbara take the red bus? (always)
Does Barbara always take the red bus?

Peter and Maria don't work on Saturday. (usually)
Peter and Maria don't usually work on Saturday.

1. Tino doesn't read the newspaper. (often)
2. Does he listen to the radio? (usually)
3. Jimmy and Linda don't eat at home. (always)
4. Do they go to Mom's Cafe? (ever)
5. Anne doesn't walk to work. (often)
6. Does she take the bus? (usually)
7. Mr. and Mrs. Bascomb don't go to the movies. (often)
8. Do they watch television? (always)
9. Do they play cards? (ever)

MARTY: Good morning, Mrs. Golo.

MRS. GOLO: What time is it, Marty?

MARTY: It's half past nine.

MRS. GOLO: That's right. You're late. You're
                always late.

MARTY: The buses are often late, too, Mrs. Golo.

MRS. GOLO: Look, Susie takes the bus,
                and she's always on time.

MARTY: But she's never early. Right,
                Mrs. Golo?

MRS. GOLO: Sit down and be quiet.

ADVERBS OF FREQUENCY

She's always on time.
____ usually _____.
____ often _____.
____ sometimes ____.
____ seldom _____.
____ never _____.

c   Add **always, usually, often, sometimes, seldom,** or **never** to the following sentences.

Examples: Marty is on time. (never)
          Marty is never on time.

          The buses are late. (often)
          The buses are often late.

1. Susie is on time. (always)
2. Mr. Brown is early. (sometimes)
3. Nancy is in a hurry. (usually)
4. Barney is worried. (never)
5. Paris is beautiful. (always)
6. Bankers are poor. (seldom)
7. Antique clocks are expensive. (usually)
8. Old books are interesting. (often)
9. Policemen are friendly. (sometimes)
10. Teachers are rich. (seldom)

d   Answer the following questions about yourself.

Example: Are you often late?
          Yes, I am. OR No, I'm never late. I'm always on time.

1. Are you always happy?
2. Are you ever sad?
3. Are you often hungry?
4. Are you often thirsty?
5. Are you usually on time?
6. Are you ever late?
7. Are your friends sometimes late?
8. Are you often in a hurry?
9. Are you usually busy?
10. Are you often tired?
11. Are you ever worried?
12. Are you ever afraid?

Jack Grubb works at night. He has a part-time job downtown. Jack isn't married and he doesn't have a family. He lives alone in a small apartment on Bond Street. Jack has an easy life; he has a lot of free time and no responsibilities. He spends most of his free time at the park across the street from his apartment. He likes the park because there are always a lot of people there. Jack often gets bored when he's alone in his apartment. But he never feels bored or lonely when he's at the park.

Jack goes to the park in the afternoon. He usually sits on a bench and reads the newspaper. Sometimes he meets interesting people in the park. They have conversations about all kinds of things, but most of the time they talk about sports and politics. Jack knows a lot about these subjects. He doesn't have a college education, but he's an intelligent man. He reads two or three books a week. At the moment, Jack isn't reading or talking. He's feeding the pigeons. He's giving them bread crumbs. Jack always has a good time in the park.

a   *Answer the following questions about the story.*

1. Does Jack work during the day?
2. Is he a family man?
3. Where does he live?
4. Does he have an easy life? Why?
5. Where does he spend his free time?
6. Why does Jack like the park?
7. What does he do there?
8. Does he ever meet interesting people in the park?
9. What do they talk about?
10. Does Jack have a college education?
11. How many books does he read a week?
12. Is he reading or talking at the moment?
13. What's he doing?

b   *Complete the following sentences using the affirmative or negative form of the verb.*

Examples: Anne and Barbara are secretaries. They (work) __*work*__ at the bank.

Barbara takes the bus to work. She (drive) *doesn't drive* a car.

1. Tino is a happy man. He (have) _____ a wonderful life.

2. The Brown family isn't rich. They (live) _____ in a big house.

3. Jimmy likes all sports. He (play)_____ football, basketball, and baseball.

4. The Golos never listen to the Rolling Stones. They (like) _____ rock music.

5. They enjoy classical music. They (listen to) _____ Mozart and Beethoven.

6. Marty is a bad student. He (do) _____ his homework.

7. I don't know the time. I (have) _____ a watch.

8. Those women are doctors. They (work) _____ in a hospital.

c   *Answer the following questions using short answers.*

Examples: Do Jimmy and Linda have a friend named Albert?
      Yes, they do.

      Does Albert play basketball?
      No, he doesn't.

1. Do Anne and Barbara work at the library?
2. Does Barbara take the bus to work?
3. Does she speak Italian?
4. Does Tino speak Italian?
5. Does he have a job at the airport?
6. Do the Browns have a big house?
7. Do they have a garden?
8. Does Otis like meat?
9. Does he like fruit and vegetables?

d   *Ask and answer questions as in the conversation on page 131.*

A: Do you have a boyfriend/girlfriend, _____ ?

B: Yes, I do. His/her name's _____ .

A: Tell me about him/her.

B. He/she is _____ .

A: Where does he/she live?

B: _____ .

A: What does he/she do?

B: _____ .

e   *Complete the following sentences using suitable prepositions.*

Example: Sam always gets up ___*at*___ seven o'clock ___*in*___ the morning.

1. Barbara works _____ the bank _____ nine _____ five.

2. She lives a long way _____ the bank.

3. The post office closes _____ twelve o'clock _____ Saturday.

4. The cat is sitting _____ the roof _____ the garage.

5. Mr. Grubb always goes _____ the park _____ the afternoon.

6. The Martinolis come _____ Italy.

7. I'm giving this book _____ Maria _____ her birthday.

8. The glasses are _____ the shelf _____ the kitchen.

f   *Answer the following questions about yourself.*

1. When do you get up in the morning?
2. What do you usually have for breakfast?
3. Where do you live?
4. Is there a park near your home? What's it like?
5. How often do you go to the park?
6. Where do you spend your free time?
7. Do you ever feel bored? lonely?
8. Where do you meet people?
9. What do you talk about with your friends?
10. Do you ever write to your friends?
11. Do you read many books? magazines?
12. What's your favorite subject?

g   *Look at the pictures and answer the following questions.*

   1. Does Barney often shave?
     No, he seldom shaves.
   2. Does Mr. Bascomb often smoke cigars?
     Yes, he usually smokes cigars.
   3. Does Anne often sing in the shower?

   4. Does Jack ever cut the grass?
   5. Do Barbara and Tino ever listen to records?
   6. Does Barbara usually take the bus to work?
   7. Does Dr. Pasto often play the piano?
   8. Do Jimmy and Linda ever go to the beach?

h   *Look at the pictures and answer the following questions.*

   1. Is Barney brushing his teeth?
     No, he isn't. He's shaving.
   2. Is Mr. Bascomb smoking?
     Yes, he is.
   3. Is Anne taking a bath?

   4. Is Jack resting?
   5. Are Barbara and Tino listening to the radio?
   6. Is Barbara walking to work?
   7. Is Dr. Pasto playing the piano?
   8. Are Jimmy and Linda going to the park?

i   *Change the following sentences as indicated.*

   Example: Otis is showing some paintings to Dr. Pasto.
            He's showing him some paintings.

   1. Peter is taking some flowers to Maria.
   2. Sam is giving a typewriter to Jimmy and Linda.
   3. Barbara is showing a photograph to Tino.
   4. We're taking some books to the students.
   5. Linda is giving a bone to the dog.
   6. Jimmy is writing a letter to his girlfriend.
   7. Albert is showing his camera to the Browns.
   8. Mrs. Golo is taking some milk to the cat.
   9. Nancy is giving a dictionary to Barney.

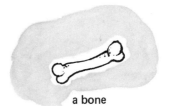

a bone

j   *Answer the following questions about yourself, using adverbs of frequency.*

   1. Do you ever get up at five o'clock?
   2. Do you often take a hot shower?
   3. Do you always brush your teeth?
   4. Do you sometimes have coffee for breakfast?
   5. Do you ever listen to the radio?
   6. Do you often read the newspaper?
   7. Do you usually wash the dishes?
   8. Do you ever leave the house in a hurry?
   9. Do you sometimes take the bus?

k   *Write a short composition about your morning routine. What do you usually do from the time you get up until you leave the house?*

VOCABULARY

alone	downtown	hamburger	pigeon	sometimes
always	during		politics	speak
		know	pop music	sports car
				subject
banana	early	late	quiet	
because	easy	live (v.)		tired
before	education	lonely		
bench	either		record (n.)	understand
bone	ever	most	responsibility	usually
bored		motorcycle		
bread crumbs	feed		Saturday	way
	feel	never	seldom	weather
			shave (v.)	word
college			sing	worried
conversation	half	often		

EXPRESSIONS OF TIME

early	on time	from nine to five
late	on Saturday	five times a week

EXPRESSIONS

a good time	in a hurry
most of the time	free time
all kinds of things	
a part-time job	

PRONUNCIATION

s		
eat<u>s</u>	help<u>s</u>	want<u>s</u>
drink<u>s</u>	work<u>s</u>	make<u>s</u>
smoke<u>s</u>	paint<u>s</u>	walk<u>s</u>

Otis never smokes or drinks.

He often walks to the park
and paints pictures.

z		
play<u>s</u>	drive<u>s</u>	call<u>s</u>
wear<u>s</u>	clean<u>s</u>	give<u>s</u>
live<u>s</u>	read<u>s</u>	show<u>s</u>

Mrs. Bascomb seldom calls her friends.

She lives in a beautiful house and
drives a big car.

iz		
watch<u>es</u>	wash<u>es</u>	cross<u>es</u>
danc<u>es</u>	brush<u>es</u>	kiss<u>es</u>
	clos<u>es</u>	

Barbara always brushes her hair
and washes her face.

She sometimes watches television.

Every morning, Mr. Brown brushes his teeth, shaves, and takes a shower.
Then he eats breakfast, reads the newspaper, and kisses his wife goodbye.

PRESENT SIMPLE Affirmative

He She	lives	
I You We They	live	in New York.

Negative

He She	doesn't (does not)	
I You We They	don't (do not)	live in New York.

Interrogative

Does	he she	
Do	I you we they	live in New York?

Short Answers

Yes,	he she	does.
	I you we they	do.

No,	he she	doesn't.
	I you we they	don't.

Question with WHAT, WHEN, WHERE, WHO

Sam wears a white hat.	What does he wear?	A white hat.
He gets up at seven o'clock.	When does he get up?	At seven o'clock.
Barbara works at the bank.	Where does she work?	At the bank.
She likes Tino Martinoli.	Who does she like?	Tino Martinoli.

ADVERBS OF FREQUENCY

They	always usually often sometimes seldom never	come	early. late. on time.

They're	always usually often sometimes seldom never		early. late. on time.

Interrogative

Do they	ever	take the bus?

Negative

They	never	take the bus.

CHAPTER TEN

Present simple vs.   **Other/another**
present   **Some/any**
continuous

a

b

a   Jimmy Brown is a student in high school. He likes his classes and gets good grades. Jimmy usually studies with his friends in the school library. He often helps them with their lessons. After school they sometimes go to the park and play football. Right now Jimmy is watching television.

1. Where does Jimmy study?
2. Is he studying now?
3. Does Jimmy help his friends with their lessons?
4. Is he helping them now?
5. Where does Jimmy go after school?
6. Is he going there now?
7. What's he doing?

b   Tino Martinoli works every day at his father's restaurant. He's very friendly and smiles at all the customers. Tino's friends often come and see him at the restaurant. They usually talk about sports. At the moment Tino is playing tennis with Barbara and he's losing.

1. What does Tino do every day?
2. Is he working now?
3. What does Tino talk about with his friends?
4. Is he talking with them now?
5. What's he doing?
6. Is he smiling?
7. Why not?

PRESENT SIMPLE

He often goes to the park.
_____ plays football.
_____ reads a book.
_____ watches TV.

PRESENT CONTINUOUS

Is he going to the park now?
_____ playing football _____?
_____ reading a book_____?
_____ watching TV _____?

c   *Make questions using the present continuous.*

Examples: Jimmy often helps his friends.
          Is he helping them now?

          They usually talk about sports.
          Are they talking about sports now?

1. They sometimes go to the park.
2. Dr. Pasto sometimes works in the garden.
3. He usually chases butterflies.
4. Barbara and Tino often play tennis.
5. She sometimes listens to records.
6. He usually reads the newspaper.
7. Jimmy and Linda often make breakfast.
8. They usually wash the dishes.
9. They sometimes clean the kitchen.

TINO: You're playing well today, Barbara.

BARBARA: I always play well, Tino.

TINO: But you don't always win.

BARBARA: I'm winning today.

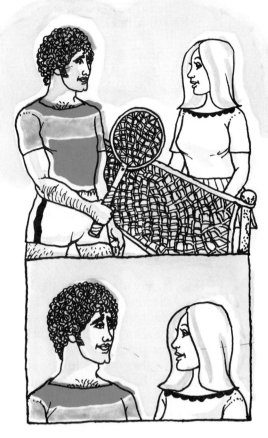

TINO: You're just lucky.

BARBARA: That's right, Tino. I'm lucky today.

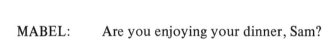

MABEL: Are you enjoying your dinner, Sam?

SAM: Of course. I always enjoy my dinner.

MABEL: But you never tell me it's good.

SAM: I'm telling you now, it's fantastic.

PRESENT SIMPLE	PRESENT CONTINUOUS
Do they always go to the park?	They're going to the park today.
_____ take sandwiches?	_____ taking sandwiches _____.
_____ play tennis?	_____ playing tennis _____.
_____ walk home?	_____ walking home _____.

d *Answer the following questions as indicated.*

Examples: Do Barbara and Tino always play tennis?
No, but they're playing tennis today.

Does Barbara always win?
No, but she's winning today.

1. Does Nancy always take the bus?
2. Does she always wear jeans?
3. Do Jimmy and Linda always clean the house?
4. Do they always help their mother?
5. Do Peter and Maria always go to the beach?
6. Do they always have hot dogs?
7. Does Mr. Bascomb always work in the garden?
8. Does Anne always go to the movies?
9. Does Otis always work at home?

jeans

PRESENT CONTINUOUS	PRESENT SIMPLE
She's reading the newspaper.	She reads the newspaper every morning.
_____ making breakfast.	____ makes breakfast _____ .
_____ drinking orange juice.	____ drinks orange juice _____ .
_____ taking a shower.	____ takes a shower _____ .

e *Change the following sentences as indicated.*

Examples: Albert is watching television. (every day)
He watches television every day.

Mr. and Mrs. Golo are going to the movies. (every week)
They go to the movies every week.

1. Dr. Pasto is chasing butterflies. (every afternoon)
2. Anne's taking a shower. (every morning)
3. Jimmy and Linda are washing the dishes. (every day)
4. Sam is cutting the grass. (every month)
5. Johnnie is painting the house. (every year)
6. Nick and Barney are playing cards. (every Saturday)
7. Nancy is cleaning the windows. (every week)
8. Peter is shaving. (every morning)
9. Jack is watching the football game. (every Sunday)

Another rainy day.

MR. BASCOMB: Goodbye, dear.

MRS. BASCOMB: Take your umbrella, John.
                  It's raining.

MR. BASCOMB: Do we have another umbrella?

MRS. BASCOMB: Yes, It's in the closet.

MR. BASCOMB: Please get it for me.

MRS. BASCOMB: Here's the other umbrella.

MR. BASCOMB: Thank you very much, dear.

ANOTHER

There's another umbrella in the closet.
_____ coat _____.
_____ hat _____.
_____ tie _____.

a   *Make sentences using **another**.*

Examples: There's a magazine on the table. (on the chair)
There's another magazine on the chair.

Barbara has a vase in her kitchen. (in her living room)
She has another vase in her living room.

1. Mr. Bascomb has a clock in his office. (in his bedroom)
2. Peter has a radio in his car. (in his office)
3. There's a library on Main Street. (on Lime Street)
4. There's a bottle on the shelf. (on the floor)
5. Nancy has a mirror in her bathroom. (in her bedroom)
6. She has a pen in her pocket. (in her desk)
7. There's a bus stop at the post office. (at the bank)
8. There's a notebook on the table. (in the desk)
9. There's a cat in the tree. (on the roof)

THE OTHER

He wants the other umbrella.
_____ coat.
_____ hat.
_____ tie.

b   *Make sentences using **one** and **the other**.*

Examples: There are two dictionaries in the bookcase. (Spanish/French)
One is Spanish and the other is French.

We have two lamps. (yellow/green)
One is yellow and the other is green.

1. Albert has two radios. (cheap/expensive)
2. Barbara has two hats. (new/old)
3. Sam has two brothers. (tall/short)
4. Nancy has two cats. (black/white)
5. There are two roses in the vase. (red/yellow)
6. There are two girls at the bus stop. (fat/thin)
7. There are two letters on the table. (from England/from France)
8. There are two libraries in the city. (on Main Street/on Lime Street)
9. There are two houses on Bunker Hill. (modern/traditional)

Peter has <u>some</u> cigarettes.

But he doesn't have <u>any</u> matches.

Maria has <u>some</u> milk.

But she doesn't have <u>any</u> sugar.

Mrs. Bascomb has <u>some</u> bread.

But she doesn't have <u>any</u> butter.

Jack has <u>some</u> bills.

But he doesn't have <u>any</u> money.

STOREKEEPER: Do you want any help, ma'am?

MABEL BROWN: Yes. I'm looking for some bananas.

STOREKEEPER: I'm sorry. There aren't any bananas left.

MABEL BROWN: Oh, that's too bad!

c   *You're in a market. Student A is the storekeeper and Student B is the customer. Ask and answer questions about the fruit in the boxes, as in the conversation above.*

A: Do you want any help, _____ ?

B: Yes, I'm looking for some _____ .

A: You're lucky. We have some nice _____ today.

    OR   I'm sorry. There aren't any _____ left.

B: Oh, that's wonderful!

    OR   Oh, that's too bad!

1. apples
2. bananas
3. pears
4. peaches
5. pineapples
6. cherries
7. oranges
8. grapes
9. lemons

Barney Field works for the Speedy Cab Company. He's an excellent driver and knows the city well. Barney enjoys his work because he meets interesting people on the job. He's very friendly and always talks with his passengers. Sometimes he tells them amusing stories about his experiences as a taxi driver. Barney often meets foreign visitors, and he gives them useful information about the city. He knows all the good restaurants, hotels, and nightclubs.

Barney takes good care of his car. He stops at Nick's Garage every day, but he seldom buys any gas there. It's very hot this afternoon, and Nick is putting water in the radiator. One of his employees is cleaning the windows and the other is putting air in the tires. Barney is drinking a cup of coffee and having a short conversation with Nick.

"My garage is a long way from the center of town," says Nick. "Why do you always bring your car here?"

"Because you're my friend," says Barney. "And I never forget my friends."

a   *Answer the following questions about the story.*

1. What company does Barney work for?
2. Why does Barney enjoy his work?
3. What does he tell his passengers?
4. Where does Barney go every day?
5. Does he often buy gas there?

6. What's Nick doing at this moment?
7. What are his employees doing?
8. What's Barney doing?
9. Is Nick's garage near the center of town?
10. Why does Barney always take his car there?

b   *Combine the following sentences, as indicated.*

Example: Barney enjoys his work. It's interesting.
         Barney enjoys his work because it's interesting.

1. He's thirsty. It's hot today.
2. Mabel is cleaning the kitchen. It's dirty.
3. People like Dr. Pasto. He's friendly.
4. Mr. Bascomb is taking his umbrella. It's raining.
5. Maria is smiling. She's happy.
6. Otis doesn't eat meat. He's a vegetarian.
7. Linda isn't eating her dinner. She isn't hungry.
8. Barbara takes the bus to work. She doesn't have a car.
9. Peter isn't working today. He's sick.

c   *Find the opposites and fill in the blanks.*

cold	ugly	cheap	white
same	late	day	weak
take	down	small	close

1. strong *weak*

2. early _____

3. night _____

4. give _____

5. large _____

6. hot _____

7. open _____

8. up _____

9. beautiful _____

10. expensive _____

11. different _____

12. black _____

d   *Answer the following questions about yourself.*

1. Do you think English is easy?
2. Do you enjoy your English class?
3. Where do you go after class?
4. What time do you go home?
5. How do you go home?
6. Do you live on a quiet street?

7. Do you ever make dinner?
8. Who washes the dishes?
9. Do you answer the phone when you're busy?
10. When do you call your friends?
11. What is your favorite time of day?
12. Do you smile when you're happy?

e   *Write a short composition about a good friend or about an interesting person you know. Who is it? What is he/she like? What does he/she do? How often do you see this person? What do you do together? What do you talk about? Why is this person special?*

f *Ask and answer questions about the pictures.*

A: What's Barney doing?
B: He's shining his shoes.
   He shines his shoes once a week.

A: What are Mr. and Mrs. Golo doing?
B: They're making the bed. They make the
   bed every morning.

1. Barney/shoes/once a week

2. Mr. and Mrs. Golo/bed/every morning

3. Maria/teeth/twice a day

4. The Bascombs/newspaper/every morning

5. Robert/girlfriend/all the time

6. Sam and Mabel/house/once a year

7. Jack/pigeons/every day

8. Barbara and Tino/tennis/every Sunday

VOCABULARY

air	customer	grade (n.)	lemon	radiator	tell
amusing		grape	lose (v.)	rainy	tennis
another	driver		lucky		tie (n.)
		high			tire (n.)
because	employee	hotel	nightclub	shame	town
	experience			stop	
care(n.)				storekeeper	useful
center	fantastic	information	other	story	
closet	foreign			study (v.)	well (adv.)
company		jeans	peach	sugar	win (v.)
conversation	gas	just	pineapple		

EXPRESSIONS

You're just lucky.

That's too bad!

Take good care of your car.

There aren't any left.

center of town

on the job

PRONUNCIATION

o

only	coat	those
open	cold	show
rose	phone	smoke
home	know	window

Don't open those envelopes.
The yellow roses are by the window.

a

clock	stop	coffee
often	pot	doctor
hot	shop	across
dog	closet	modern

Tom often stops at the coffee shop.
He eats a lot of hot dogs.

The post office opens at nine o'clock.
Joe wants a cold bottle of Coke.

SOME/ANY Affirmative

She has	some	apples. oranges. bread. butter.
They have		

Negative

She doesn't have	any	apples. oranges. bread. butter.
They don't have		

Interrogative

Does she have	any	apples? oranges? bread? butter?
Do they have		

Short Answers

Yes,	she does. they do.

No,	she doesn't. they don't.

There's a	lamp clock vase table	in the living room.

ANOTHER

There's another	lamp clock vase table	in the bedroom.

ONE   THE OTHER

There are two	lamps. clocks. vases. tables.

One	lamp clock vase table	is old and the other	(lamp) (clock) (vase) (table)	is new.

PRESENT SIMPLE

He	always usually often sometimes seldom	goes to the movies.

PRESENT CONTINUOUS

Is he going to the movies now?

CHAPTER ELEVEN

''To need''   Some/any/one as
Can   pronouns

a

b

a Peter is worried. He's a long way from the city and the gas tank is empty. He needs some gas. He's looking for a gas station, but there aren't any nearby.

1. Why is Peter worried?
2. What does he need?
3. What about oil?
4. What's Peter looking for?
5. Are there any gas stations nearby?

b Anne is coming from the shower. Her hair is wet and she's holding a towel around her. Anne doesn't have many clothes; she always wears the same dress. She needs a new one. She also needs a new pair of shoes.

1. Where's Anne coming from?
2. Is her hair wet or dry?
3. What's she holding around her?
4. Does Anne have many clothes?
5. What does she need?

AFFIRMATIVE

Anne needs some shoes.
She _____.
Jack _____.
He _____.

The children need some clothes.
We _____ .
You _____ .
I _____ .

c *Look at the pictures below and answer the following questions.*

1. What does Barney need?
   He needs some socks.
2. What does Mrs. Golo need?
3. What does Mr. Bascomb need?
4. What does Maria need?
5. What does Barbara need?
6. What does Tino need?
7. What does Mrs. Bascomb need?
8. What does Jack need?

STOREKEEPER: What do you need today, Mrs. Brown?

MRS. BROWN: I need some potatoes and tomatoes.

STOREKEEPER: Do you need any onions?

MRS. BROWN: No, I already have some, thank you.

MR. BASCOMB: What's the matter, sonny?

BOBBY: I don't have any money.

MR. BASCOMB: How much do you need?

BOBBY: I need two dollars.

MR. BASCOMB: Here. Take this.

BOBBY: Thank you, mister.

INTERROGATIVE

Does Mrs. Brown need any onions?
_____ she _____?
_____ Barney _____?
_____ he _____?

Do you need a shopping cart?
___ they _____?
___ we _____?
___ the Golos _____?

d *Make questions as indicated.*

Examples: they/food _Do they need any food?_

she/coffeepot _Does she need a coffeepot?_

1. you/stamps _____

2. she/typewriter _____

3. Jimmy/books _____

4. your friends/money _____

5. Nancy/mirror _____

6. we/shampoo _____

7. he/lamp _____

8. you/matches _____

9. they/desk _____

NEGATIVE

Mrs. Brown doesn't need any onions.
She _____.
Barney _____.
He _____.

I don't need a shopping cart.
They _____.
We _____.
The Golos _____.

e *Make negative sentences as indicated.*

Examples: we/soap
We don't need any soap.

Fred/towel
Fred doesn't need a towel.

soap

shopping cart

toothpaste

1. They/eggs
2. I/milk
3. She/dictionary
4. You/envelopes
5. The Browns/clock
6. Otis/typewriter
7. I/pencils
8. We/toothpaste
9. Maria/umbrella

1   Mrs. Brown is a good cook.

She can make spaghetti.
_____ chocolate cake.
_____ banana bread.
_____ fried chicken.

2   Mr. Brown has a big appetite.

He can eat a whole chicken.
_____ a chocolate cake.
_____ three hamburgers.
_____ five hot dogs.

3   Jimmy is a fine athlete.

He can play basketball.
_____ football.
_____ baseball.
_____ tennis.

4   Nancy is very intelligent.

She can speak French.
_____ German.
_____ Spanish.
_____ English.

AFFIRMATIVE

Jimmy can play tennis.
He _____ .
Linda _____ .
She _____ .

They can play the piano.
You _____ .
We _____ .
I _____ .

a   *Answer the following questions about yourself.*

1. What languages can you speak?
2. What languages can your parents speak?
3. What sports can you play?
4. What musical instruments can you play?
5. What songs can you sing?
6. What dances can you do?
7. What games can you play?
8. What dishes can you make?
9. How many eggs can you eat?

checkers

chess

violin

flute

trumpet

guitar

drums

piano

cards

TINO: What kind of movies
             do you like, Barbara?

BARBARA: I like French movies.

TINO: Can you speak French?

BARBARA: No, but I can
             understand it.

SAM BROWN: Can you make a banana
                 cake today?

MABEL BROWN: No, I can't.

SAM BROWN: Why not?

MABEL BROWN: I don't have any bananas.

b   *Ask and answer questions as indicated.*

Example 1: speak French?
Student A: **Can you speak French?**
Student B: **Yes, I can.** OR **No, I can't.**

1. _____ speak French?

2. _____ play the violin?

3. _____ repair a car?

4. _____ make pizza?

5. _____ type?

6. _____ ride a bicycle?

7. _____ drive a truck?

8. _____ dance?

9. _____ play basketball?

It's Wednesday night at the Martinoli Restaurant. Tino is taking orders from Mr. and Mrs. Hamby. They're regular customers at the restaurant. Mr. Hamby wants a big plate of spaghetti with meat sauce. For dessert he wants some Italian ice cream. His wife can't have spaghetti or ice cream. She's watching her weight. Mrs. Hamby is ordering a bowl of vegetable soup for dinner. She doesn't want any dessert.

"There's no vegetable soup," says Tino. "But I can bring you some chicken soup."

"Wonderful," says Mrs. Hamby. "I love chicken soup."

"This is a fine restaurant," says Mr. Hamby. "Except for one thing."

"What's that?" says Tino.

"There's no music."

"You need some Italian music," says Mrs. Hamby. "And some pictures of Italy on the wall."

"That's a good idea," says Tino. "I have some pictures of Venice at home. I can use them."

"Wonderful," says Mrs. Hamby. "I love Venice."

a   *Answer the following questions about the story.*

1. What night is it?
2. What's Tino doing?
3. Do the Hambys often go to the Martinoli Restaurant?
4. What does Mr. Hamby want for dinner?
5. What does Mrs. Hamby want?
6. Does she want any dessert?
7. Why not?
8. What kind of soup does Tino have?
9. What does the restaurant need?

b   *Change the following sentences as indicated.*

Examples: There isn't any vegetable soup.   We don't have any clean glasses.
           There's no vegetable soup.   **We have no clean glasses.**

1. There aren't any green vegetables.   6. There aren't any eggs.
2. There isn't any fruit.   7. We don't have any coffee.
3. We don't have any bananas.   8. We don't have any clean cups.
4. We don't have any milk.   9. There isn't any sugar.
5. There isn't any bread.

c   *Make questions as indicated.*

Example: Barbara/French
          Can Barbara speak French?

1. Mrs. Golo/spaghetti   6. Dr. Pasto/the piano
2. Albert/a whole cake   7. Anne/a bicycle
3. Linda/the guitar   8. Tino/tennis
4. Mr. Bascomb/a truck   9. Nancy/Japanese
5. Maria/the tango

d   *Answer the following questions about your favorite restaurant.*

1. **What's the name of your favorite restaurant? Where is it?**
2. Why do you like it? How is it different from other restaurants?
3. What kind of food do they serve? Is the menu always the same?
4. Are the waiters/waitresses friendly?
5. What kind of people go there? How do they dress?
6. Is the restaurant clean? noisy? expensive?
7. Do they have music? What kind?
8. Is it a romantic place? Do they put flowers or candles on the tables?
9. Is it a good place for conversation? Do you often go there with friends?
10. Do you ever meet new people there?

e   *Write a short composition about your favorite restaurant.*

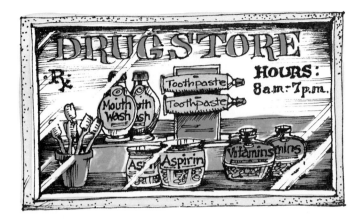

READ AND PRACTICE

You need some aspirin. It's 6:30 p.m.

A: Where can I get some aspirin?

B: At the drugstore.

A: Is it still open?

B: Yes, it's open until seven.

You need a ruler. It's 5:45 p.m.

A: Where can I get a ruler?

B: At the stationery store.

A: Is it still open?

B: No, it closes at five-thirty.

You need a lock. It's 8:30 a.m.

A: Where can I get a lock?

B: At the hardware store.

A: Is it open now?

B: No, it opens at nine.

f   *Ask and answer questions using the information below.*

1. You need some pencils. It's 8:45 a.m.
2. You need a hammer. It's 6:20 p.m.
3. You need some toothpaste. It's 6:40 p.m.
4. You need a paintbrush. It's 8:30 a.m.
5. You need some vitamins. It's 9:00 a.m.
6. You need a pen. It's 5:10 p.m.

7. You need some mouthwash. It's 7:30 p.m.
8. You need some nails. It's 9:15 a.m.
9. You need a notebook. It's 6:00 p.m.
10. You need a toothbrush. It's 6:30 p.m.
11. You need some envelopes. It's 5:45 p.m.
12. You need some paint. It's 8:50 a.m.

VOCABULARY

already	cook (n.)	hold (v.)	pair	shampoo	trumpet
animal			parent	socks	type (v.)
appetite	dessert	language	poetry	song	
athlete	drums	love (v.)		sonny	use (v.)
	dry		regular	swim	
baseball		nearby	repair (v.)		violin
	empty	need (v.)		tango	
can (v.)	except		samba	tank	Wednesday
checkers		oil	same	toothpaste	weight
chess	flute	onion	sauce	towel	wet
clothes		order (v.)			

EXPRESSIONS

What's the matter?

PRONUNCIATION

eyr				**er**		
h<u>air</u>	p<u>ear</u>	v<u>e</u>ry		h<u>er</u>	mod<u>er</u>n	w<u>or</u>k
w<u>ear</u>	ch<u>air</u>	<u>air</u>port		sk<u>ir</u>t	d<u>ir</u>ty	dinn<u>er</u>
c<u>are</u>	wh<u>ere</u>	rep<u>air</u>		und<u>er</u>	w<u>or</u>d	aft<u>er</u>
th<u>ere</u>	th<u>eir</u>	diction<u>ar</u>y		count<u>er</u>	danc<u>er</u>	l<u>ear</u>n

Where's their dictionary?   Her hamburger is on the counter.
There's a pear on the chair.   The singer and dancer want dessert after dinner.

Mary is wearing a dirty skirt.
Their university is very modern.

NEED Affirmative

He She	needs		pencils.
I You We They	need	some	paper.

Negative

He She	doesn't need		pencils.
I You We They	don't need	any	paper.

Interrogative

Does	he she		pencils?
Do	I you we they	need any	paper?

Short Answers

Yes,	he she	does.
	I you we they	do.

No,	he she	doesn't.
	I you we they	don't.

CAN Affirmative

He She I You We They	can	swim.

Negative

He She I You We They	can't (cannot)	swim.

Interrogative

Can	he she I you we they	swim?

Short Answers

Yes,	he she I you we they	can.

No,	he she I you we they	can't.

NOT ANY/NO

There aren't any cookies in the jar.
They don't have any money.

There are	no	cookies in the jar.
They have	no	money.

PRONOUNS

Linda needs some envelopes.
Jimmy doesn't have any toothpaste.
I need a dictionary.

She doesn't have	any.
He needs	some.
I don't have	one.

CHAPTER TWELVE

Review

a   *Answer the following questions about the story.*

   1. Where are Peter and Maria?
   2. What kind of day is it?
   3. What does Peter smell?
   4. How much time do they have before the movie starts?
   5. What can Maria see in the pond?
   6. Are there any fish in Marty's bucket?
   7. What does Peter say about a good fisherman?
   8. Why is Marty happy to give Peter his fishing pole and worms?
   9. What does the sign say?
  10. Why can't Peter read the sign?
  11. What does the officer say to Peter?
  12. Why is the officer surprised that Peter and Maria are going to a movie?

b   *Ask and answer questions as indicated.*

Example 1:   at the library
Student A: **What can you do at the library?**
Student B: **You can read, study, get information,**
                     borrow books, etc.

1. at the park   4. at a party
2. at the zoo   5. downtown
3. at the beach   6. at home

Example 2:   with lemons, water, and sugar
Student C: **What can you do with lemons, water, and sugar?**
Student D: **You can make lemonade.**

1. with ice, fruit, and cream
2. with bread, ham, and cheese
3. with some wood, a hammer, and nails
4. with a pen and paper
5. with a paintbrush and some paint
6. with $5.00   with $50.00   with $5,000.00

c   *Answer the following questions about yourself.*

   1. How often do you go to the movies?
   2. Is there a movie theater near your house?
   3. What do you do in the afternoon?
   4. How often do you see your friends? Where do you meet? What do you do?
   5. What do you do when a friend asks you for money? What about a stranger?
   6. What do you do when you're tired? hungry? sick? bored? lonely?
   7. Do you often help other people? How?
   8. Do you have any friends from foreign countries? What language(s) do they speak?
   9. Is there someone special in your life? Who is it? What do you like about this person?
  10. Describe your life. Is it easy? hard? sad? wonderful?

d *Write a sentence for each picture using **can't**.*

1. *You can't fish in the pond.*

2. *You can't feed the animals at the zoo.*

3. _____

4. _____

5. _____

6. _____

7. _____

8. _____

c   *Answer the following questions using adverbs of frequency.*

Examples: Does Barney often talk with his passengers? (yes/always)
Yes, he always talks with his passengers.

Do Anne and Barbara drive to work? (no/never)
No, they never drive to work.

1. Does Barbara play tennis? (yes/often)
2. Does Jimmy study at home? (yes/sometimes)
3. Do Mr. and Mrs. Brown watch television? (no/seldom)
4. Do they listen to the radio? (yes/usually)
5. Does Albert ever play basketball? (no/never)
6. Do Nick and Barney read the newspaper? (yes/often)
7. Does Jimmy help his friends? (yes/always)
8. Do Mr. and Mrs. Golo work in the garden? (yes/sometimes)
9. Does Jack ever get up at seven o'clock? (no/never)

f   *Complete the following sentences using possessive adjectives and possessive pronouns.*

Examples: I'm writing a letter to ___*my*___ sister.

Don't take that pen. It isn't ___*yours*___.

1. I wash _____ car every week. How often do you wash _____?

2. What do the Browns have in _____ garage?

3. We clean _____ apartment once a week. They clean _____ once a month.

4. Albert is asking Linda for _____ telephone number.

5. We're taking the typewriter because it's _____.

6. Mr. Bascomb says those envelopes are _____. Give them to him.

7. I never forget _____ birthday. Why do you always forget _____?

8. Please give this book to Anne. It's _____.

9. Jimmy always takes _____ notebook when he goes to school.

g   *Ask and answer questions as indicated.*

Example: go to the market
Student A: **How often do you go to the market?**
Student B: **I go to the market every day/twice a week, etc.**
OR I never go to the market.

1. take a shower
2. wash your hair
3. shine your shoes
4. change your socks
5. clean your room
6. make dinner
7. wash the dishes
8. drink coffee/tea
9. brush your teeth
10. go to the dentist/doctor
11. get a haircut
12. exercise/play a sport

h   *Make negative questions.*

Examples: Can you read?   Are they working today?
          Can't you read?   **Aren't they working today?**

1. Is Susie doing her homework?   6. Can you talk with Linda?
2. Does she have a dictionary?   7. Is she at home?
3. Can Marty write a letter?   8. Do we have her phone number?
4. Are they in class?   9. Are we going to a movie tonight?
5. Do they like school?   10. Does Linda have any money?

i   *Change the following sentences as indicated.*

Examples: Peter needs some matches.   They need a car.
          He doesn't have any.   **They don't have one.**

1. Linda needs some toothpaste.   6. You need some large towels.
2. I need some shampoo.   7. Maria needs a teapot.
3. Jack needs a raincoat.   8. She needs some sugar.
4. He needs some tennis shoes.   9. Wickam City needs a good hotel.
5. We need a dictionary.

j   *Ask and answer questions using the verb* **to need***.*

Example: babies
Student A: **What do babies need?**
Student B: **They need milk.**

1. flowers   6. you
2. cars   7. your family
3. tires   8. this school
4. a tired person   9. this town
5. a sick person

k   *Read and practice. Look at the picture on page 181.*

A: Where can I get some detergent?   C: Where can I get a sandwich?

B: At the market.   D: At Mom's Cafe.

A: Is there a market nearby?   C: Where is Mom's Cafe?

B: Yes, there's one on Franklin Avenue,   D: It's on Main Street, between the bank
   across from the church.   and the theater.

Ask and answer questions as in the dialogues above.

1. some roses   6. an umbrella
2. some stamps   7. some paper plates
3. a cup of coffee   8. a dictionary
4. a map of the city   9. some traveler's checks
5. some aspirin   10. a haircut

map   traveller's
                       checks

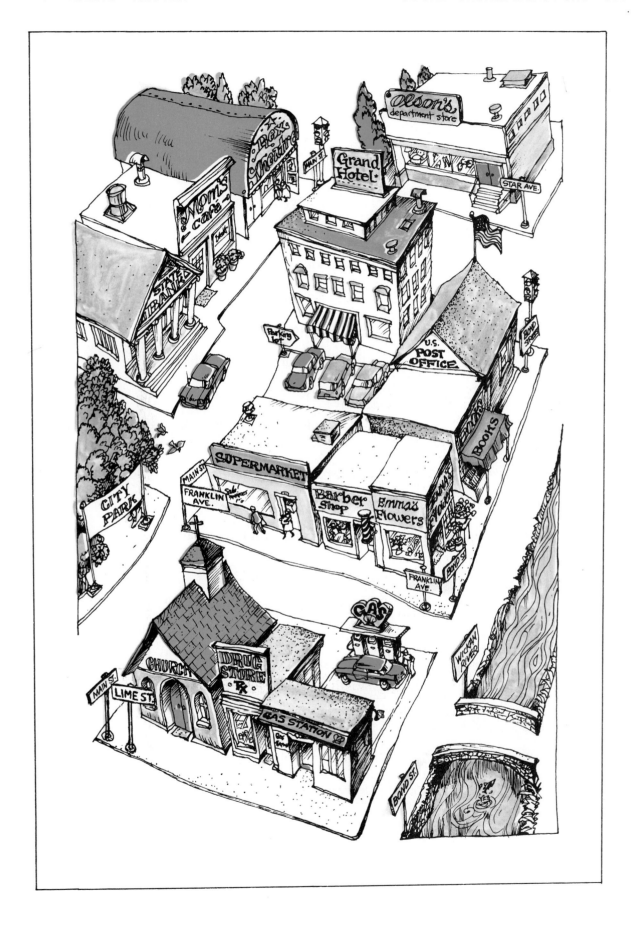

l   Complete the following sentences using *there's a, there's some* or *there are some.*

Examples: *There are some* glasses on the shelf.

There's some ice cream in the kitchen.

1. _____ roses in the garden.

2. _____ bread on the table.

3. _____ photographs in the desk.

4. _____ football in the closet.

5. _____ soup in the kitchen.

6. _____ clock in the living room.

7. _____ dishes in the sink.

8. _____ sugar next to the coffeepot.

9. _____ vase by the window.

10. _____ tomato juice in the can.

m   *Complete the following sentences using the present simple or the present continuous.*

Examples: Barbara always *takes* the bus to work. (take)

She *is waiting* at the bus stop right now. (wait)

1. Nick is busy today. He _____ at the garage. (work)

2. The garage _____ at 8 a.m. (open) It _____ at 6 p.m. (close)

3. Nick _____ his job. (like) He _____ it's interesting. (think)

4. Come on. Our friends _____ for us. (wait)

5. Take your umbrella. It _____. (rain)

6. Mr. Bascomb is in the kitchen. He _____ breakfast. (make)

7. He usually _____ coffee with his breakfast. (drink)

8. He _____ his coffee with cream and sugar. (like)

9. Mrs. Bascomb is sitting in the living room. She _____ a letter. (write)

10. Look at the cat! It _____ on the sofa. (sleep)

n   *Look at the pictures and complete the sentences with correct prepositions and object pronouns.*

1. The students are _in_ the classroom.
   Mrs. Golo is standing *in front of them* .

2. Marty is writing _____ his desk.
   Mrs. Golo is standing _____ .

3. There's a vase _____ the table.
   Linda is putting some flowers _____ .

4. Anne is _____ the movies.
   A tall man is sitting _____ .

5. Mr. Bascomb is _____ his car.
   His wife is sitting _____ .

6. The boys are _____ the bus stop.
   An old woman is _____ .

7. There's a car _____ the garage.
   Nick is _____ .

8. Susie is _____ her bicycle.
   Marty is standing _____ .

o   *Change the following sentences using object pronouns.*

Example: She's getting <u>the umbrella</u> for <u>her husband</u>.
   She's getting <u>it</u> for <u>him</u>.

1. He's showing <u>his paintings</u> to <u>Dr. Pasto</u>.
2. I'm taking <u>these oranges</u> to <u>Maria</u>.
3. She's getting <u>the magazines</u> for <u>you and me</u>.
4. He's giving <u>the typewriter</u> to <u>the students</u>.
5. We're buying <u>the radio</u> for <u>Anne</u>.
6. She's bringing <u>the letters</u> to <u>Mr. Bascomb</u>.
7. He's buying <u>the statue</u> for <u>Tino and me</u>.
8. I'm giving <u>that clock</u> to <u>my friends</u>.
9. We're taking <u>this lamp</u> to <u>Mrs. Golo</u>.

p   *Answer the following questions about yourself.*

1. How often do you go to parties?
2. What kind of parties do you like?
3. Who makes dinner at your house? What time do you have dinner?
4. Do you have interesting conversations at dinner? What do you talk about?
5. Do you usually have a cup of coffee after dinner?
6. Do you often go out at night? Where do you go? What do you do?
7. Do you need money to have a good time? What is your idea of a good time?
8. What are some things you need? Do you ever buy things you don't need?
9. What do you often think about?

VOCABULARY

bucket	fisherman	map	perfume	start (v.)
		marvelous	pond	
catch	glasses			traveler's checks
catfish		nothing	raincoat	
	haircut			without
downtown	happiness	officer		wood
			smart	
exercise (v.)	luck	party	smell (v.)	zoo

EXPRESSIONS

Let's go.	lots of	No fishing.
I'm glad.	Mmm . . .	Sure, mister.

TEST

1. What is the color_____ your kitchen?

   a. for   c. in
   b. of   d. at

2. Do you have a television _____ your living room?

   a. on   c. to
   b. at   d. in

3. Mr. Grubb works_____ night.

   a. in   c. at
   b. during   d. for

4. There's a park across the street _____ the church.

   a. of   c. to
   b. from   d. for

5. Are there many trees _____ your street?

   a. at   c. on
   b. for   d. in

6. What do you want _____ lunch?

   a. for   c. to
   b. of   d. from

7. Call the waiter. Ask _____ for the menu.

   a. he   c. her
   b. him   d. them

8. Those aren't your matches. Don't take _____.

   a. them   c. this
   b. they   d. it

9. Anne and I are busy. Don't talk to _____ now.

   a. her   c. us
   b. me   d. them

10. He's giving _____ some magazines.

    a. she   c. to her
    b. for her   d. her

11. I have _____ birthday in July.

    a. my   c. mine
    b. me   d. your

12. The Browns are cleaning _____ house.

    a. they   c. there
    b. their   d. they're

13. That typewriter belongs to Barbara. It's _____.

    a. her   c. hers
    b. to her   d. she

14. I'm in a hurry. I'm _____ for work.

    a. early   c. late
    b. on time   d. ready

15. Anne isn't working today because she's _____.

    a. sick   c. bored
    b. at home   d. lonely

16. Can Tino _____ Italian?

    a. tell   c. talk
    b. say   d. speak

17. Your perfume _____ good.

    a. looks   c. feels
    b. smells   d. works

18. Mr. Poole doesn't have any friends. He's a _____ man.

    a. happy   c. lucky
    b. friendly   d. lonely

19. How does Maria go to work?

    a. By car.   c. In the morning.
    b. On time.   d. At the bus stop.

20. You can get stamps at the _____.

    a. gas station   c. post office
    b. library   d. bank

21. Oranges are my favorite _____ .

    a. fruit   c. color
    b. vegetable   d. drink

22. Linda is _____ . She wants a glass of water.

    a. busy   c. hungry
    b. tired   d. thirsty

23. Please wash the dishes. They're _____ .

    a. clean   c. old
    b. new   d. dirty

24. _____ does Peter go to work?
    At nine o'clock.

    a. Why   c. When
    b. Where   d. How

25. _____ does he like his job?
    Because it's interesting.

    a. Why   c. When
    b. Where   d. How

26. Anne's coat is ten years old.
    She _____ a new coat.

    a. has   c. likes
    b. needs   d. wears

27. We always _____ at Mom's Cafe.

    a. are eating   c. eat
    b. eats   d. feed

28. I usually _____ dinner at six.

    a. has   c. am having
    b. having   d. have

29. The boys _____ football now.

    a. plays   c. are playing
    b. playing   d. play

30. A good fisherman always _____ fish.

    a. catch   c. catching
    b. catches   d. is catching

31. Sam is in the kitchen.
    He _____ coffee.

    a. is making   c. make
    b. makes   d. making

32. Marty is a bad student.
    He _____ his homework.

    a. does not   c. doesn't do
    b. doesn't make   d. don't do

33. Can you help me?

    a. No, I don't.   c. No, I can.
    b. No, I'm not.   d. No, I can't.

34. _____ some stamps in the desk.

    a. It has   c. There
    b. They're   d. There are

35. Albert is hungry. He wants
    _____ sandwich.

    a. other   c. some
    b. another   d. more

36. The _____ dictionary is in the bookcase.

    a. other   c. different
    b. another   d. other one

37. Jane doesn't have a watch.
    She needs _____ .

    a. it   c. any
    b. one   d. another

38. There's _____ bread on the table.

    a. a   c. some
    b. any   d. one

39. Miss Hackey is _____ .

    a. actress   c. an actress
    b. a actress   d. one actress

40. I'm American. What's your _____ ?

    a. composition   c. language
    b. personality   d. nationality

CHAPTER THIRTEEN

Simple past: **Tag questions**
    ''to be''   **Ordinal numbers**

TODAY

YESTERDAY

WEATHER REPORT

Today all of Europe is having good weather.
But yesterday it was rainy in Moscow.
_____cold in Paris.
_____windy in Rome.
_____cloudy in London.

a Nancy Paine often travels to Europe.
Yesterday she was in Moscow. She was
unhappy because the weather was bad.
It was rainy. Today Nancy is in London.
The weather is good. It's sunny. Nancy
is very happy.

  1. Where was Nancy yesterday?
  2. Why was she unhappy?
  3. Where is Nancy today?
  4. What's the weather like?

b Mr. and Mrs. Golo are on vacation in
Europe. Yesterday they were in Paris and
the weather was terrible. It was very cold
and damp. But today they're in Rome and
the weather is fantastic. It's sunny and
warm.

  1. Where were Mr. and Mrs. Golo yesterday?
  2. What was the weather like?
  3. Where are Mr. and Mrs. Golo today?
  4. What's the weather like?

c *Complete the sentences about the pictures using these adjectives:* **sad**, **thirsty**, **tired**, **cold**, **angry**, **busy**, **afraid**, **happy**, **hungry**.

1. I was *tired* .

2. You were _____ .

3. He was _____ .

4. They were _____ .

5. We were _____ .

6. She was _____ .

7. You were _____ .

8. I was _____ .

9. They were _____ .

Peter is returning from a trip to Spain. Johnnie Wilson is meeting him at the airport.

JOHNNIE: How was your trip, Peter?

PETER: It was wonderful.

JOHNNIE: Were the people friendly?

PETER: Yes, they were very friendly.

JOHNNIE: What was the weather like?

PETER: It wasn't very good. There was
            a lot of rain.

JOHNNIE: What were the hotels like?

PETER: Very nice. Everything was good
            except the weather.

AFFIRMATIVE

Jimmy was at the park yesterday.	They were at the movies last Friday.
He _____ .	You _____ .
Linda _____ .	We _____ .
I _____ .	The students _____ .

d   *Ask and answer questions as in the conversation on page 191. You can use these adjectives to describe the weather and the hotels:* **good,** *very nice,* **wonderful, fantastic, bad,** *not very nice,* **awful, terrible.**

Student A: How was your trip, _____ ?

Student B: It was _____ .

Student A: Were the people friendly?

Student B: _____ .

Student A: What was the weather like?

Student B: _____ .

Student A: What were the hotels like?

Student B: _____ .

NEGATIVE

Jimmy wasn't at home yesterday.	They weren't in class last Friday.
He _____ .	You _____ .
Linda _____ .	We _____ .
I _____ .	The students _____ .

e   *Answer the following questions in the negative, as indicated.*

Examples: Where were the students last Friday? (in class)
   I don't know. They weren't in class.

   Where was Miss Paine yesterday? (at work)
   I don't know. She wasn't at work.

1. Where were your friends last weekend? (at home)
2. Where was Maria yesterday? (at the hospital)
3. Where was she last night? (at her apartment)
4. Where were Anne and Barbara last Monday? (at the office)
5. Where was Nick yesterday? (at the garage)
6. Where were the children yesterday afternoon? (at school)
7. Where was Mr. Bascomb last Wednesday? (at the bank)
8. Where were Barbara and Tino last Sunday? (at the park)
9. Where was Tino yesterday? (at the restaurant)

BARBARA: Where were you yesterday?

TINO: I was at the beach.

BARBARA: Were you with anyone?

TINO: Yes, I was with a friend named Gina.

BARBARA: Was she young and beautiful?

TINO: No, she wasn't. She was old and ugly.

BARBARA: Are you telling me the truth, Tino?

TINO: Yes, of course.

INTERROGATIVE

Was Tino at the beach yesterday?   Were you at the park last week?
____ he _____?   _____ they_____?
____ Barbara _____?   _____ we _____?
____ she_____?   _____ the Browns _____?

f   *Ask and answer questions using* **was** *and* **were**. *Use past time expressions such as* **yesterday,
last night, this morning, etc.**

Example: alone
Student A: **Were you alone last night?**
Student B: **Yes, I was. OR No, I wasn't. I was with some friends.**

1. at home
2. at the park
3. tired
4. hungry
5. at the library
6. at the post office
7. in a hurry
8. worried
9. sick
10. angry
11. busy
12. free

I was sick.

THE FOUR SEASONS

Summer

fall

winter

spring

MONTHS OF THE YEAR

January	April	July	October
February	May	August	November
March	June	September	December

DAYS OF THE WEEK

Monday   Tuesday   Wednesday   Thursday   Friday   Saturday   Sunday

ORDINAL NUMBERS

1st	first		16th	sixteenth
2nd	second		17th	seventeenth
3rd	third		18th	eighteenth
4th	fourth		19th	nineteenth
5th	fifth		20th	twentieth
6th	sixth		21st	twenty-first
7th	seventh		22nd	twenty-second
8th	eighth		23rd	twenty-third
9th	ninth		24th	twenty-fourth
10th	tenth		25th	twenty-fifth
11th	eleventh		26th	twenty-sixth
12th	twelfth		27th	twenty-seventh
13th	thirteenth		28th	twenty-eighth
14th	fourteenth		29th	twenty-ninth
15th	fifteenth		30th	thirtieth

a   *Answer the following questions about yourself.*

1. When is your birthday?
2. When is your mother's birthday? father's birthday?
3. When is New Year's Day?
4. What is your favorite holiday? When is it?
5. When is the first day of summer? winter?
6. What is your favorite day of the week?
7. What is your favorite month?
8. What is your favorite season? Why do you like it?
9. What is special about spring? summer? winter?

Dr. Pasto was in South America last March. Here is his travel itinerary.

MARCH						
Sunday	Monday	Tuesday	Wednesday	Thursday	Friday	Saturday
			1 *Bogotá*	2	3	4 *Quito*
5	6	7 *Lima*	8	9 *La Paz*	10	11
12 *Santiago*	13	14	15 *Buenos Aires*	16	17	18 *São Paulo*
19	20 *Rio de Janeiro*	21	22	23 *Brasília*	24	25
26 *Caracas*	27	28 *Panama City*	29	30	31	

b   *Look at the calendar and answer the following questions about Dr. Pasto's trip.*

Example: When was Dr. Pasto in Bogotá?
         He was in Bogotá on March first, second, and third.

1. When was he in Quito?
2. When was he in Lima?
3. When was he in La Paz?
4. When was he in Santiago?
5. When was he in Buenos Aires?
6. When was he in São Paulo?
7. When was he in Rio de Janeiro?
8. When was he in Brasília?
9. When was he in Caracas?
10. When was he in Panama City?

SANDY: Hi, Peter. It's a beautiful day, isn't it?

PETER: Yes, it is.

SANDY: You're going to the beach, aren't you?

PETER: Yes, I am.

SANDY: You weren't at the beach yesterday, were you?

PETER: No, I wasn't.

SANDY: You always go by car, don't you?

PETER: Yes, I do.

SANDY: I can't go with you, can I?

PETER: Yes, you can. Get in.

TAG QUESTIONS

You're going to the beach, aren't you?
They're _____, _____ they?
She's _____, _____ she?
He's _____, _____ he?

c *Add tag questions to the following sentences.*

Examples: He always goes by car.
He always goes by car, doesn't he?

You were late yesterday.
You were late yesterday, weren't you?

1. They often take the bus.
2. She's a doctor.
3. He can play tennis.
4. You're going to the airport.
5. We have their address.
6. They work at the bank.
7. She was at the movies last night.
8. We're good dancers.
9. You like sports.

d *Ask and answer tag questions as indicated.*

Example: student/study

Student A: You're a good student aren't you?
Student B: **Yes, I am.**   OR   **No, I'm not.**

Student A: You study a lot, don't you?
Student B: **Yes, I do.**   OR   **No, I don't.**

1. dancer/dance
2. singer/sing
3. artist/paint
4. student/study
5. typist/type
6. cook/cook

TAG QUESTIONS

You weren't at the beach yesterday, were you?
They _____, _____ they?
She wasn't _____, was she?
He _____, _____ he?

e *Add tag questions to the following sentences.*

Examples: I can't go with you.
I can't go with you, can I?

He doesn't have a telephone.
He doesn't have a telephone, does he?

1. They aren't at home.
2. The bank wasn't open yesterday.
3. You don't have a dictionary.
4. He isn't taking the bus.
5. I don't know her.
6. You aren't a teacher.
7. She doesn't want another job.
8. They weren't at the party.
9. He can't swim.

f *Ask and answer tag questions as indicated.*

Example: student/study

Student A: You aren't a very good student, are you?

Student B: **Yes, I am.**   OR   **No, I'm not.**

Student A: You don't study much, do you?

Student B: **Yes, I do.**   OR   **No, I don't.**

1. dancer/dance
2. singer/sing
3. artist/paint
4. student/study
5. typist/type
6. cook/cook

It's Tuesday morning, June 25. Mr. Bascomb is at the bank. He's talking with some businessmen from Chicago. They're representatives of a large toy company. Mr. Bascomb and his guests are discussing plans for the construction of a toy factory in Wickam City. Mr. Bascomb thinks it's a good idea. He always encourages the establishment of new businesses in his city.

"It's good for the economy," says Mr. Bascomb. "New businesses provide more jobs for the people and money for the city."

Mr. Bascomb works long hours and seldom takes a vacation. It's very unusual when he doesn't come to work. Yesterday was an unusual day. Mr. Bascomb wasn't at work. He was at home. He was sick in bed all day. But he wasn't alone. His wife and his dog were there with him.

a　*Answer the following questions about the story.*

    1. What day is it?
    2. Where is Mr. Bascomb?
    3. Who is he talking with?
    4. What kind of company do they represent?
    5. What are they discussing?
    6. Why does Mr. Bascomb encourage new businesses?
    7. How often does Mr. Bascomb take a vacation?
    8. Was he at work yesterday?
    9. Was he sick?
  10. Was he alone?

b　*Give short answers to the following questions.*

    Example:　You have a bicycle, don't you?
              Yes, I do.　OR　No, I don't.

    1. You like classical music, don't you?
    2. You're a good dancer, aren't you?
    3. You can play the guitar, can't you?
    4. You're at home every night, aren't you?
    5. You need a dictionary, don't you?
    6. You don't speak Russian, do you?
    7. You aren't thinking about the weekend, are you?
    8. You weren't at the park last Sunday, were you?
    9. You can't drive a car, can you?
  10. You don't have a watch, do you?

c　*Ask and answer questions about the pictures on page 201. Use past time expressions like* **yesterday, yesterday afternoon, last night, this morning, last Sunday,** *etc. You can use any suitable adjectives.*

    Example 1:　Barbara and Tino/musicians

    Student A:　**Where were Barbara and Tino last night?**
    Student B:　**They were at a jazz concert.**

    Student A:　**What were the musicians like?**
    Student B:　**They were excellent (wonderful, marvelous).**

    Example 2:　Gloria/coffee

    Student C:　**Where was Gloria this morning?**
    Student D:　**She was at Joe's Coffee Shop.**

    Student C:　**What was the coffee like?**
    Student D:　**It was terrible (very bad, awful).**

    3. Peter and Sandy/weather　　　　　6. Mr. and Mrs. Golo/movie
    4. Anne/weather　　　　　　　　　　7. Jimmy and Linda/water
    5. Albert/pastries　　　　　　　　　　8. Mr. Bascomb/models

1.

2.

3.

4.

5.

6.

7.

8.

d *Complete the following sentences with **at, on, in** or no preposition.*

Examples: He usually takes his vacation ___*in*___ August.

The post office closes ___*at*___ five p.m.

Our club meetings are ___*on*___ Wednesday.

Are you busy _____ this week?

1. It's always hot _____ the summer.

2. We often go to the beach _____ the weekend.

3. Where were you _____ last Saturday?

4. Anne goes to work _____ eight o'clock _____ the morning.

5. She was at the library _____ yesterday afternoon.

6. She never leaves the house _____ night.

7. Peter's birthday is _____ July 9th.

8. He was in Europe _____ 1984.

9. You always call me _____ the wrong time.

10. I'm busy _____ the afternoon.

11. Let's have our meeting _____ tomorrow morning.

12. I can't see you _____ Tuesday.

e *Answer the following questions about the street you live on.*

1. What are the houses like on your street?
2. Are there many trees on your street? cafes? shops?
3. Is your street quiet or noisy? wide or narrow?
4. What kind of people live on your street? Are there many families with children?
5. What are your neighbors like? Are they friendly?
6. Is your street safe or dangerous at night?
7. What kind of transportation do people use on your street? Do most people drive their cars, take the bus, or ride bicycles?
8. What is unusual or different about your street? In other words, how is your street special?
9. Do you like your street? Why or why not?

f *Write a short composition about the street you live on.*

VOCABULARY

alone	eleventh	June	pastry	sixteenth	truth
anyone	encourage		plan (n.)	sixth	Tuesday
April	establishment	last (adj.)	president	spring	twelfth
awful			provide	summer	twentieth
	factory	March		sunny	
beer	fall (n.)	market	rain (n.)	swim	unhappy
	February	May	report (n.)		
calendar	fifteenth	model	represent	tenth	vacation
cloudy	fifth		representative	terrible	
construction	fourteenth	narrow	return (v.)	third	warm
	fourth	neighbor		thirteenth	was
damp	Friday	nineteenth	safe	thirtieth	weekend
discuss		ninth	second	Thursday	were
	guest	noisy	September	toy	windy
economy		November	seventeenth	transportation	winter
eighteenth	itinerary		seventh	travel (v.)	
eighth	January	October	sick	trip	yesterday

EXPRESSIONS

go by car   get in   sick in bed   a lot of

Past Time Expressions

yesterday	last night	last weekend
yesterday morning	last Friday	last month
yesterday afternoon	last week	last year

PRONUNCIATION

a				ae		
sock	often	economy		can	sandwich	bank
shop	pocket	politics		hat	dancer	stamp
job	across	doctor		black	glass	plant
box	bottle	coffee		apple	Spanish	shampoo

The doctor often walks to his office.   Sam can understand Spanish.
Tom wants some hot coffee.   Nancy is asking for a glass of apple juice.

Dottie has a lot of black socks.
Dan is washing the pots and pans.

Past of TO BE   Affirmative

He She I	was	
You We They	were	in Paris yesterday.

Negative

He She I	wasn't (was not)	
You We They	weren't (were not)	in Paris yesterday.

Interrogative

Was	he she I	
Were	you we they	in Paris yesterday?

Short Answers

Yes,	he she I	was.
	you we they	were.

No,	he she I	wasn't.
	you we they	weren't.

TAG QUESTIONS

It's a beautiful day,	isn't it?	There aren't any matches,	are there?
They're going to the beach,	aren't they?	He isn't working today,	is he?
You have an umbrella,	don't you?	They don't like football,	do they?
She was at the movies,	wasn't she?	You weren't at the party,	were you?
He can play the piano,	can't he?	She can't drive a truck,	can she?
He likes music,	doesn't he?	He doesn't have a telephone,	does he?

CHAPTER FOURTEEN

Simple past: affirmative

Simple past: negative and interrogative

Yesterday . . .

Otis walked to the park.

He watched a basketball game.

He played chess.

He listened to some musicians.

Last night . . .

The movie started at seven o'clock.

It ended at nine o'clock.

Last Sunday . . .

1

Anne sang for Barbara and Tino.

2

Dr. Pasto found an African butterfly.

3

Nancy bought a motorcycle.

4

Linda made a birdhouse.

5

Peter drove to the beach.

6

He took his dog with him.

7

They swam in the ocean.

8

Peter lost his car keys.

SIMPLE PAST TENSE OF REGULAR VERBS

She worked in the garden.
___ washed the car.
___ cleaned the kitchen.
___ prepared dinner.
___ rested after dinner.

a   *Complete the following sentences using the simple past tense.*

Example: They (walk) to the library yesterday.
              They walked to the library yesterday.

1. Dr. Pasto (paint) his garage last Sunday.
2. Sam (help) him.
3. They (talk) about the weather.
4. We (enjoy) our dinner last night.
5. Mabel (prepare) chicken and fried potatoes.
6. I (look) at some magazines after dinner.
7. Maria (show) us some pictures of Paris last week.
8. She (live) in France for a year.
9. She (like) the women's clothes.

SIMPLE PAST TENSE OF IRREGULAR VERBS

They got up at eight o'clock.
____ took a shower.
____ had breakfast.
____ read the newspaper.
____ went to work.

b   *Make sentences as indicated.*

Example: Peter went to the beach.   (I/to the park)
              I went to the park.

1. You got up at nine o'clock.   (We/at nine thirty)
2. She had a hamburger for lunch.   (Albert/a hot dog)
3. I lost my notebook.   (You/your pen)
4. We saw a movie.   (Our friends/a football game)
5. He took a shower.   (She/a bath)
6. Maria bought a vase.   (I/a chair)
7. You went to the movies.   (We/to the museum)
8. He found a butterfly.   (They/a cat)
9. Mrs. Golo made a chocolate cake.   (I/a sandwich)

c

d

c   Sam Brown lives in California. Last month he went to New York and visited his brother Bob. They talked about old times and looked at family photographs. Sam stayed in New York for a week. He enjoyed his visit very much.

1. Where does Sam Brown live?
2. Where did he go last month?
3. Who did he visit there?
4. What did they talk about?
5. What did they look at?
6. How long did Sam stay in New York?
7. Did he enjoy his visit?

d   Peter Smith had a good time when he was in Spain. He took his camera with him and got some interesting pictures of Madrid. He thought it was a beautiful city. On his last night there he went to a nice little restaurant called La Cocinita. He had chicken and potatoes for dinner and listened to flamenco music. Before he left Spain, Peter bought some postcards for his friends in Wickam City. Johnnie Wilson met him at the airport when he came home.

1. Did Peter have a good time when he was in Spain?
2. What did he take with him?
3. Did he get pictures of Barcelona or Madrid?
4. What did he think of Madrid?
5. Where did he go on his last night there?
6. What did he have for dinner?
7. Did he listen to flamenco music or rock music?
8. What did Peter buy for his friends before he left Spain?
9. Who met him at the airport when he returned to Wickam City?

AFFIRMATIVE

Peter went to a famous restaurant.
You _____.
They_____.
We _____.
She _____.
I _____.

e   *Complete the following sentences using the simple past tense.*

Example: Jimmy and Linda (go) to the art museum.
Jimmy and Linda went to the art museum.

1. They (take) the bus.
2. They (meet) their friends at the museum.
3. They (see) some beautiful paintings.
4. Jimmy (like) the paintings from England.
5. Linda (enjoy) everything.
6. They (stay) at the museum for an hour.
7. They (eat) lunch at Joe's Snack Bar.
8. Linda (have) a bowl of fruit salad.
9. Jimmy (buy) some candy.

JIMMY: Did you have a good time in New York, dad?

SAM: Yes, I did, Jimmy.

JIMMY: What did you and Uncle Bob do?

SAM: We talked about old times.

JIMMY: Did he show you the city?

SAM: Yes, we visited the Statue of Liberty and the United Nations.

JIMMY: Did you see any movies?

SAM: No, but we saw a very interesting play.

JIMMY: When can we go to New York?

SAM: Next year, Jimmy. You and Linda can go with me.

a   *Make negative sentences as indicated.*

1. Sam went to New York.
   He didn't go to Chicago.

2. Linda made a birdhouse.
   _____ a doghouse.

3. Nancy bought a motorcycle.
   _____ a car.

4. Otis watched a basketball game.
   _____ a football game.

5. Dr. Pasto found a butterfly.
   _____ a bird.

6. Anne played the guitar.
   _____ the piano.

7. ____ to the beach.
   _____ to the park.

8. He took his dog with him.
   _____ his cat with him.

ALBERT: Did you go out Saturday night, Linda?

LINDA: Yes, I went to a party.

ALBERT: What did you do there?

LINDA: We sang and danced all night.

ALBERT: Did they have any food?

LINDA: Yes, they had some delicious
           pastries.

ALBERT: I'm sorry I missed the party.

INTERROGATIVE	SHORT ANSWER FORM	
Did Linda have a good time?	Yes, she did.	No, she didn't.
___ Albert _____ ?	___ , he ___ .	___ , he _____ .
___ they _____ ?	___ , they__ .	___ , they ____ .
___ you _____ ?	___ , I ____ .	___ , I _____ .

b *Answer the following questions using the short answer form.*

Examples: Did Linda stay home Saturday night?
No, she didn't.

Did she go to a party?
Yes, she did.

1. Did she go with Albert?
2. Did she wear jeans?
3. Did she dance at the party?
4. Did they have pastries?
5. Did Sam go to Texas last month?
6. Did he visit his brother?
7. Did they see the Statue of Liberty?
8. Did they go to a movie?
9. Did Sam stay in New York for a month?
10. Did he enjoy his visit?

c *Ask and answer questions as indicated. Use past time expressions like **yesterday**, **yesterday afternoon**, **last night**, **this morning**, **last Sunday**, etc.*

Example: see a movie
Student A: **Did you see a movie last week?**
Student B: **Yes, I did. OR No, I didn't.**

1. go to the park
2. stay home
3. watch television
4. listen to the radio
5. play basketball
6. do your homework
7. take the bus
8. see your friends
9. buy some fruit
10. wash the dishes
11. read the newspaper
12. get a letter

d *Ask and answer questions as in the conversation below.*

Student A: Did you have a good time Saturday night/yesterday/last weekend, _____ ?

Student B: Yes, I did. OR No, I didn't.

Student A: Where did you go?

Student B: _____ .

Student A: What did you do (there)?

Student B: _____ .

Last Sunday Albert and Jimmy went to the beach. There were hundreds
of people there. Jimmy played volleyball and swam in the ocean. But Albert
just sat on the beach and watched the girls. It was a hot day and Albert was
very thirsty. He wanted a cold drink. Unfortunately, the only restaurant at
the beach was closed. The temperature was 90 degrees and Albert was very
uncomfortable. Finally he saw a girl with a large picnic basket. It was Jane
Garner, a friend from college. Albert carried the basket for her, and she gave
him a drink. Five minutes later Jimmy came and sat with them. They ate and
drank and had a good time.

a   *Answer the following questions about the story.*

1. Where did Albert and Jimmy go last Sunday?
2. How many people were there?
3. What did Jimmy do?
4. What did Albert do?
5. What was the weather like?

6. What did Albert want?
7. Were there any restaurants open?
8. Who did Albert see on the beach?
9. What did she have?
10. What did she give Albert?
11. What happened five minutes later?

b   *Make questions with **who**, **what**, or **where**.*

Examples: Albert went <u>to the beach</u>.   He saw <u>Jane Garner</u>.
          Where did he go?   **Who did he see?**

She gave him <u>a drink</u>.
What did she give him?

1. Barney went <u>to the market</u> yesterday.
2. He bought <u>some apples and pears</u>.
3. He met <u>Nancy</u> at one o'clock.
4. He gave her <u>an apple</u>.
5. They went <u>to Mom's Cafe</u> for lunch.

6. They ordered <u>fried chicken</u>.
7. They saw <u>Tino</u>.
8. He talked about <u>Barbara</u>.
9. She made <u>a cake</u> yesterday.

c   *Answer the following questions as indicated.*

Examples: What did Jane give Albert? (a drink)   What did Sam bring his wife? (some flowers)
          She gave <u>him</u> a drink.   **He brought <u>her</u> some flowers.**

1. What did Peter buy <u>Maria</u>? (some chocolates)
2. What did she bring <u>her friends</u>? (a banana cake)
3. What did they give <u>Otis</u>? (a record player)
4. What did the students bring <u>Mrs. Golo</u>? (a cat)
5. What did she give <u>the cat</u>? (some milk)
6. What did Jack take <u>the Browns</u>? (some old magazines)
7. What did they give <u>Jack</u>? (an old lamp)
8. What did Barney show <u>the tourists</u>? (the university)
9. What did he bring <u>Nancy</u>? (some roses)

d   *Ask and answer questions as indicated.*

Example: corn
Student A: **Is corn your favorite vegetable?**
Student B: **Yes, it is. OR No. Peas are my favorite (vegetable).**

1. red
2. apples
3. coffee
4. ice cream
5. January

6. English
7. football
8. dogs
9. summer
10. roses

corn   peas

e *Change the following sentences to the simple past tense.*

1. Mr. Jones lives in San Francisco.
2. He works at the post office.
3. Every morning he gets up at 7:30 and takes a shower.
4. He usually has coffee and eggs for breakfast.
5. Mr. Jones always goes to work at 8:30.
6. He takes the bus to work.
7. He seldom meets people on the bus.
8. Mr. Jones is a quiet man.
9. He doesn't often talk to strangers.

f *Give short answers to the following questions.*

Example: Linda and Albert are friends, aren't they?
             Yes, they are. OR No, they aren't.

1. Peter drives a sports car, doesn't he?
2. Anne and Barbara work at the garage, don't they?
3. Barbara doesn't have a boyfriend, does she?
4. Tino is a pilot, isn't he?
5. This book has 300 pages, doesn't it?
6. Sam didn't go to Chicago, did he?
7. He has a brother in New York, doesn't he?
8. They didn't visit the Statue of Liberty, did they?
9. They went to a play, didn't they?

g *Complete the following sentences.*

Example: Peter went to the bank ___*to borrow some money.*___

1. Anne stopped at the post office _____

2. Did your brother go to the market _____

3. I'm going to the barber shop _____

4. My friends are going home _____

5. Mr. Bascomb is stopping at the drugstore _____

6. Did you go to the library _____

7. Maria went to the hardware store _____

8. We're going to the park _____

9. Sam is stopping at the flower shop _____

h *Look at the pictures and answer the following questions.*

1. Where was Johnnie yesterday?
   He was at home.
2. Where were Anne and Nancy?
   They were at the park.
3. Where was Mrs. Golo?

4. Where was Sam?
5. Where were Maria and Peter?
6. Where was Mr. Bascomb?
7. Where was Jimmy?
8. Where were Barbara and Tino?

i *Answer the following questions about the pictures.*

1. Was Johnnie at home yesterday?
   Yes, he was.
2. Were Anne and Nancy at the beach?
   No, they weren't. They were at the park.
3. Was Mrs. Golo at the museum?

4. Was Sam at the garage?
5. Were Peter and Maria at the movies?
6. Was Mr. Bascomb at the pet shop?
7. Was Jimmy at the record shop?
8. Were Barbara and Tino at the movies?

j *Answer the following questions.*

1. What did Johnnie do yesterday?
   He painted the house.
2. What did Anne and Nancy do?
   They played chess.
3. What did Mrs. Golo do?

4. What did Sam do?
5. What did Maria and Peter do?
6. What did Mr. Bascomb do?
7. What did Jimmy do?
8. What did Barbara and Tino do?

k *Answer the following questions.*

1. Did Johnnie go to the movies yesterday?
   No, he didn't. He painted the house.
2. Did Anne and Nancy play chess?
   Yes, they did.
3. Did Mrs. Golo read a book?

4. Did Sam watch television?
5. Did Maria and Peter go to the opera?
6. Did Mr. Bascomb buy a chair?
7. Did Jimmy listen to records?
8. Did Barbara and Tino play tennis?

l *Answer the following questions about yourself.*

1. Did you see a movie last week?
2. Where did you go last weekend? How did you go there?
3. What did you do yesterday? Did you see your friends?
4. Did you study last night? watch television?
5. What time did you go to bed?
6. What time did you get up this morning?
7. What did you have for breakfast?
8. Did you read the newspaper this morning?
9. What did you do after breakfast?

m *Write a short composition about an interesting day. What happened to you? Where were you? Who were you with?*

VOCABULARY

African	degree	finally	later	see	uncomfortable
after	delicious	find		sorry	unfortunately
		flamenco	miss (v.)	start (v.)	
basket	end (v.)		musician	stay	visit (v.)
	enter	hundred			visit (n.)
carry (v.)			peas	temperature	volleyball
chess	film	key	play (n.)		
corn					

EXPRESSIONS

old times   all night   all day

PRONUNCIATION

id

painted	needed	waited
rested	repeated	started
wanted	visited	ended

He painted the house and visited his sister.

The movie started at seven and ended at nine.

She repeated the question and waited for an answer.

d

opened	prepared	rained
closed	loved	stayed
cleaned	showed	called
played	smiled	entered

It rained last Sunday and she stayed home.

She opened the door and he entered.

He showed her the photograph and she smiled.

t

asked	crossed	washed	talked
danced	walked	liked	chased
laughed	worked	looked	watched

Linda laughed and danced all night.

They watched television and talked about football.

Jack walked to the library and looked at magazines.

They worked, rested, and played cards.

She painted the house, washed the car, and cleaned the kitchen.

He liked, loved, and needed his dog.

SIMPLE PAST   Affirmative

He She I You We They	walked drove took the bus	to class last week.

Negative

He She I You We They	didn't (did not)	walk drive take the bus	last week.

Interrogative

Did	he she I you we they	walk drive take the bus	last week?

Short Answers

Yes,	he she I you we they	did.

No,	he she I you we they	didn't.

SIMPLE PAST   Irregular Verbs

He	bought ate took found had	some candy yesterday.

Regular Verbs

They	danced talked	at the party.
	worked lived	in New York.

Question with WHERE, WHEN, WHO, WHAT

Anne went to the park. She left at 12 o'clock. She met Nancy. They played chess.	Where did she go? When did she leave? Who did she meet? What did they play?	To the park. 12 o'clock. Nancy. Chess.

CHAPTER FIFTEEN

Future with "going to"   **Adverbs of manner**

a

b

c

d

a   Peter is packing his suitcase. He's preparing for another trip. Tomorrow he's going to travel to France. He's going to stay in Paris for a week. He's going to visit the Eiffel Tower.

    1. What's Peter doing?
    2. What's he going to do tomorrow?
    3. How long is he going to stay in Paris?
    4. What's he going to do there?

b   Albert is picking up the phone. He's going to call Linda. He's going to invite her to a movie. He's going to drive his father's car.

    1. What's Albert doing?
    2. Who's he going to call?
    3. Is he going to invite her to a movie or a concert?
    4. Is he going to take a taxi or drive his father's car?

c   Mrs. Brown went to the market this morning. She bought some chocolate, eggs, flour, and sugar. She's going to make a chocolate cake for Jimmy. It's his birthday tomorrow. He's going to have a party.

    1. Where did Mrs. Brown go this morning?
    2. What did she buy?
    3. What's she going to make?
    4. When's Jimmy going to have his party?

d   Tino is at the florist's. He's looking at some flowers. He's going to buy some carnations. He's going to give them to Barbara.

    1. Where's Tino?
    2. What's he looking at?
    3. What's he going to buy?
    4. Who's he going to give them to?

AFFIRMATIVE

Peter's going to stay in Paris.	We're going to visit London.
He's _____.	They're_____.
Mary's _____.	You're _____.
She's _____.	I'm _____.

e   *Answer the following questions about the stories above.*

    Example: Is Peter going to travel <u>to England</u>?
               No, he's going to travel to France.

    1. Is he going to stay in Paris <u>for a month</u>?
    2. Is he going to visit <u>the Tower of London</u>?
    3. Is Albert going to call <u>Jane</u>?
    4. Is he going to invite her <u>to a concert</u>?
    5. Is he going to drive <u>his mother's car</u>?
    6. Is Mrs. Brown going to make <u>an orange cake</u>?
    7. Is Jimmy going to have his birthday party <u>next week</u>?
    8. Is Tino going to buy <u>some roses</u>?
    9. Is he going to give them <u>to Maria</u>?

MABEL BROWN: What are you going to do this
                weekend?

SAM BROWN: I'm going to plant some banana
                trees.

MABEL BROWN: Where are you going to plant
                them?

SAM BROWN: In back of the house.

MABEL BROWN: What are you going to do
                then?

SAM BROWN: I'm going to sit down and
                relax.

JIMMY: What are you going to do tonight?

LINDA: I'm going to see a movie with Albert.

JIMMY: With Albert? But he doesn't have
          a car.

LINDA: He's going to drive his father's car.

INTERROGATIVE

Is Linda going to stay home?   Are they going to play tennis?
_ she _____ ?   ___ you _____ ?
_ Albert _____ ?   ___ we _____ ?
_ he _____ ?   ___ the Browns _____ ?

f   *Make questions with **going to**.*

    Example: Sam is going to stay home. (watch television)
                Is he going to watch television?

1. He's going to work in the back yard. (plant apple trees)
2. Albert and Linda are going to see a movie. (take the bus)
3. They're going to have dinner after the movie. (eat at home)
4. Peter is preparing for another trip. (visit Germany)
5. He's packing his suitcase. (take his camera)
6. He's going to visit France. (stay in Nice)
7. Tino is going to see Barbara tonight. (give her some flowers)
8. They're going to have a party next week. (invite Peter and Maria)
9. Maria is working at the hospital today. (have lunch there)

NEGATIVE

Linda isn't going to stay home.   They aren't going to play tennis.
She _____ .   You _____ .
Albert _____ .   We _____ .
He _____ .   The Browns _____ .

g   *Make negative sentences with **going to**.*

    Example: Sam is going to work in the back yard. (in the house)
                He isn't going to work in the house.

1. He's going to plant banana trees. (apple trees)
2. Albert and Linda are going to see a movie. (a play)
3. They're going to take the car. (the bus)
4. They're going to have dinner after the movie. (before the movie)
5. They're going to eat in a Mexican restaurant. (at home)
6. Peter is going to visit France. (Germany)
7. He's going to stay in Paris. (in Nice)
8. Tino is going to see Barbara tonight. (Maria)
9. They're going to play chess. (cards)

a   Barbara is a good secretary. She types quickly and accurately. She listens carefully and doesn't make mistakes. Barbara works very well.

    1. What kind of secretary is Barbara?
    2. How does she type?
    3. Does she listen carefully?
    4. Does she make mistakes?
    5. How does she work?

b   Anne is a bad secretary. She types slowly and makes a lot of mistakes. She doesn't listen carefully and works badly.

    1. What kind of secretary is Anne?
    2. How does she type?
    3. Does she make mistakes?
    4. Does she listen carefully?
    5. How does she work?

ADVERBS OF MANNER

She's a good typist.	She types well.
_____ bad ____ .	_____ badly.
_____ slow ____ .	_____ slowly.
_____ quick ____ .	_____ quickly.
_____ careful __ .	_____ carefully.

c   *Change the following sentences, using adverbs.*

Examples: Anne is a slow worker.   *She works slowly.* _____

           Dr. Pasto is a good speaker. *He speaks well.* _____

1. Jack is a good cook. _____

2. He's a dangerous driver. _____

3. Fred is a careful writer. _____

4. He's a slow reader. _____

5. Mrs. Golo is a bad dancer. _____

6. She's a good singer. _____

7. Barbara is a quick typist. _____

8. She's a careful driver. _____

MR. BASCOMB: You're working slowly, Miss Jones.

ANNE JONES: That's because I'm working carefully.

MR. BASCOMB: But you make a lot of mistakes.

ANNE JONES: I know, Mr. Bascomb.

MR. BASCOMB: Perhaps I don't speak clearly.

ANNE JONES: No, I understand you perfectly.

MR. BASCOMB: Then what's the problem?

ANNE JONES: I don't know, Mr. Bascomb.

d *Look at the pictures and make a sentence about each one using an adverb.*

1. (loud) Mrs. Golo *speaks loudly* .

2. (soft) Barbara _____

3. (dangerous) Jack _____

4. (careful) Barney _____

5. (good) Otis and Gloria _____

6. (beautiful) Anne _____

7. (quick) Albert _____

8. (slow) Fred _____

e *Answer the following questions about the pictures as indicated.*

1. Does Mrs. Golo speak loudly?
   Yes, she does.
2. Does Barbara speak loudly?
   No, she doesn't. She speaks softly.
3. Does Jack drive carefully?
4. Does Barney drive carefully?
5. Do Otis and Gloria dance badly?
6. Does Anne sing beautifully?
7. Does Albert eat quickly?
8. Does Fred read quickly?

f *Make questions with* **how.**

Example: Barney drives carefully. (Nancy)
          How does Nancy drive?

1. Anne sings beautifully. (Barbara)
2. Linda writes well. (Jimmy)
3. Fred dresses badly. (Barney)
4. Barbara speaks softly. (Mrs. Golo)
5. Jack drives dangerously. (Peter)
6. Mabel cooks well. (Nancy)
7. Albert types slowly. (Jimmy)
8. Gloria and Otis dance well.
   (Peter and Maria)
9. Barbara works quickly. (Anne)

g *Describe how you do the following activities, using the adverbs* **quickly, slowly, carefully, well, badly, loudly, softly,** *and* **beautifully.**

Examples: sing
          I sing well.
          walk
          I walk quickly.

1. dance
2. play chess
3. read
4. walk
5. eat
6. write
7. speak
8. dress
9. work
10. sing

There's a big crowd of people at the Odeon Theater tonight. They're waiting anxiously for Ula Hackey, the famous Hollywood actress. She's going to attend the premiere of her new film, *Sweet Summer*. Everyone is very excited. Miss Hackey is coming now. She's waving happily to the crowd. The man next to her is a television announcer. He's going to ask Miss Hackey some questions about her new film. There are some photographers following the actress. They're going to take pictures of her for the newspapers. She's a very popular star. After the film, Miss Hackey is going to sign autographs and talk to the people.

a *Answer the following questions about the story.*

1. Who are the people waiting for?
2. Why is she at the Odeon Theater tonight?
3. Who is she waving to?
4. Who is the man next to Miss Hackey?
5. What's he going to do?

6. Who are the men following the actress?
7. What are they going to do?
8. Why do they want pictures of Miss Hackey?
9. What is she going to do after the film?

b *Make questions with **going to.***

Example: Maria/take a bath
Is Maria going to take a bath?

1. she/wash her hair
2. she/meet Peter tonight
3. they/see a play
4. Peter/drive his car
5. he/come at eight o'clock
6. he/bring some flowers
7. Maria/wear a red dress
8. she/take a coat
9. they/eat at the Martinoli Restaurant

c *Make negative sentences with **going to.***

Example: I/wear a hat
I'm not going to wear a hat.

1. He/come to the party
2. They/watch television
3. She/study in the library
4. You/take the bus
5. I/write a letter
6. She/live in New York
7. We/visit the museum
8. They/go to the park
9. He/play baseball

d *Answer the following questions about yourself.*

1. What are you going to do after class?
2. Are you going to walk home?
3. What are you going to do tonight?
4. Who are you going to see?
5. What are you going to have for dinner?

6. What are you going to do tomorrow?
7. What time are you going to get up?
8. Are you going to see your friends tomorrow?
9. What are you going to do this weekend?

e *Complete the following sentences using the word **because.***

Example: Barbara takes the bus to work *because she doesn't have a car.*

1. Tino isn't working today _____

2. Anne is taking her umbrella _____

3. I'm happy _____

4. I like my job _____

5. Linda isn't eating her dinner _____

6. Sam is cleaning the house _____

7. Mabel is resting _____

8. The teacher is unhappy _____

f   *Complete the dialogue.*

OTIS: Hi, Gloria.

GLORIA: Hello, Otis.

OTIS: What are you going to do tonight?

GLORIA: I'm going _____ .

OTIS: Oh, really? What's the name of the movie?

GLORIA: It's called _____ .

OTIS: Is it a comedy?

GLORIA: No. _____ .

OTIS: Who's in it?

GLORIA: _____ .

OTIS: Is she a good actress?

GLORIA: Yes. _____ .

OTIS: Where's the movie playing?

GLORIA: _____ .

OTIS: Is that on Maple Street?

GLORIA: No. _____ .

OTIS: What time does the first show start?

GLORIA: _____ . Why don't you come?

OTIS: Sure, why not? I like love stories, too.

Now talk about a movie you're going to see.

g   *Write a short composition about what you're going to do this weekend. Are you going to see a movie? Have a party? Go to the beach?*

h *Complete the following sentences using suitable adjectives. There can be more than one suitable adjective for each sentence.*

Example: I don't like this chair. It's _ugly (too big) (uncomfortable)_ .

1. Put on your coat. It's _____ outside.

2. Be _____ when you cross the street.

3. You need an umbrella on _____ days.

4. There's nobody with that woman. She's _____ .

5. Is there any food in the refrigerator? I'm _____ .

6. You're going to like this cake. It's _____ .

7. Please wash the dishes. They're _____ .

8. Joe is a _____ man. He's married to a beautiful woman.

9. She loves coffee. It's her _____ drink.

10. She puts ketchup in her coffee. Isn't that _____ ?

11. Marty never comes on time. He's always _____ .

12. We all make mistakes. Nobody's _____ .

i *Complete the following sentences using these adverbs: **happily, slowly, badly, carefully, quickly, well, immediately, loudly, softly, warmly**. Use each adverb only once.*

Example: Jimmy ate _quickly_ because he was in a hurry.

1. People usually speak _____ in the library.

2. Mr. Bascomb walked _____ up the stairs. He was very tired.

3. He can't see very _____ without his glasses.

4. We always dress _____ on cold days.

5. Anne really needs dancing lessons. She dances very _____ .

6. The people next door talk very _____ . You can hear them through the walls.

7. The children are playing _____ in the front yard. They're all laughing.

8. I need you right away. Please come _____ .

9. The streets are dangerous. Drive _____ .

VOCABULARY

accurately	carnation	invite	premiere	soft
actress	clearly			speaker
announcer	concert	loud	quick	star
anxiously	crowd		quickly	suitcase
attend		mistake		
autograph	excite		reader	then
		pack (v.)	relax	tomorrow
	famous	perfectly		typist
back	florist	perhaps	show (n.)	
badly	flour	phone	sign (v.)	worker
	follow	photographer	slow	writer
careful		popular	slowly	
carefully	happily			

EXPRESSIONS

for a week	Why not?
for a month	

Future Time Expressions

tonight	this weekend
tomorrow	next week
tomorrow morning	next month
tomorrow night	next year

PRONUNCIATION

	e			ey	
hotel	left	President	grade	radiator	favorite
weekend	pet	September	shape	education	dangerous
forget	attend	seldom	late	conversation	game
chess	when	expression	table	mistake	sale

The President went to Mexico in September.
Fred seldom gets dressed before seven.

Take the vase from the table.
Jane made a cake for David.

The famous chess player seldom made a mistake.
She never lost a game of chess.

GOING TO   Affirmative

He She	's (is)		see a movie.
I	'm (am)	going to	play tennis.
You We They	're (are)		visit Paris.

Negative

He She	isn't 's not (is not)		see a movie.
I	'm not (am not)	going to	play tennis.
You We They	aren't 're not (are not)		visit Paris.

Interrogative

Is	he she		see a movie?
Am	I	going to	play tennis?
Are	you we they		visit Paris?

Short Answers

Yes,	he she	is.
	I	am.
	you we they	are.

No,	he she	isn't.
	I	'm not.
	you we they	aren't.

He's going to	work in London. leave next month. write to his wife. buy a suitcase.

Question with WHERE, WHEN, WHO, WHAT

Where's he going to work? When's he going to leave? Who's he going to write to? What's he going to buy?	In London. Next month. His wife. A suitcase.

Question with HOW

How does she	work? drive?

ADVERBS OF MANNER

She	works drives	well. badly. slowly. quickly. carefully.

CHAPTER SIXTEEN

Review

NANCY'S JOURNEY

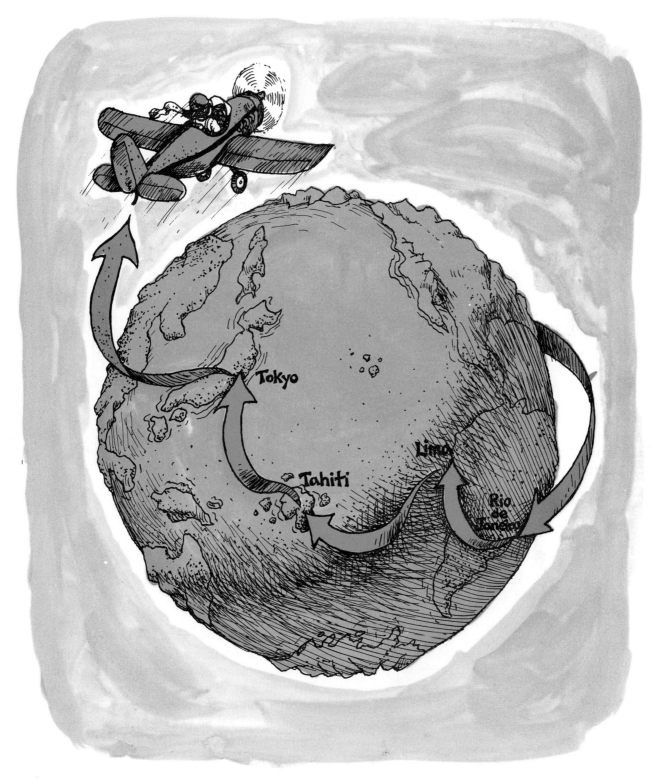

Last summer Nancy Paine flew around the world. She started in New York and made her first stop in Rio de Janeiro. Rio is a wonderful city and Nancy made some good friends there. They taught her a few words of Portuguese and she learned the samba.

After a week in Rio, Nancy continued her journey. She flew over some very high mountains called the Andes and landed in Lima, Peru. She walked around the capital and took photographs of the beautiful old churches. Nancy left Peru on a fine, sunny day. She traveled across the Pacific Ocean to the island of Tahiti.

It was a very long trip, more than two thousand miles. But the weather was good, and she didn't have any problems. Nancy loved the people of Tahiti, and she had a good time there. She sailed a small boat and swam in the ocean every day. The sun was always hot and the beaches were beautiful. Everything was perfect.

After two weeks Nancy got back in her plane and left for Japan. She stayed in Tokyo for a couple of days, in a small hotel near the center of the city. She found a very nice teahouse across the street from her hotel. Nancy enjoyed the lovely gardens there. She also admired the traditional clothes of the Japanese women.

Nancy's next stop was Moscow, Russia. She had some rough weather on the way. But Nancy is an expert pilot, and she arrived at her destination without any serious trouble. In Moscow she bought a fur coat and saw some folk dancers.

The last stop on Nancy's journey was Paris, the "City of Light." She visited some friends in the Latin Quarter, and they took her to a fine restaurant near the river Seine. Nancy ate frog legs and drank some delicious white wine. Her friends asked a lot of questions about her travels, and she told them everything. It was quite a journey.

a   *Answer the following questions about Nancy's journey.*

1. What did Nancy Paine do last summer?
2. Where did she start?
3. Where did she make her first stop?
4. What did Nancy learn in Rio?
5. Where did she go after Brazil?
6. What did she do in Lima?
7. What was Nancy's next stop?
8. What did she do in Tahiti?
9. Did she have a good time there?
10. Where did Nancy go after Tahiti?
11. How long did she stay in Tokyo?
12. What did she find across the street from her hotel?
13. What did Nancy admire about the Japanese women?
14. What was her next stop?
15. What did she buy there?
16. What did she see?
17. Where did Nancy go after Moscow?
18. Who did she visit there?
19. Where did they take her?
20. What did she drink?

b   *Make questions with **what . . . like**.*

Examples: weather/Paris   hotels/Japan
            What was the weather like in Paris?   **What were the hotels like in Japan?**

1. restaurants/Rome   6. museums/New York
2. beer/Germany   7. people/Mexico City
3. cafes/France   8. food/Korea
4. parks/England   9. transportation/China
5. music/Brazil

c   *Answer the following questions as indicated.*

Example: Does Anne listen to the radio? (No/seldom)
           No, she seldom listens to the radio.

1. Does she play the guitar? (Yes/often)
2. Does Barney stop at Nick's garage? (Yes/always)
3. Do they talk about politics? (No/seldom)
4. Do they play cards? (Yes/sometimes)
5. Does Mrs. Golo feed the cat? (Yes/always)
6. Does she cut the grass? (No/never)
7. Do Mr. and Mrs. Bascomb go to the theater. (Yes/often)
8. Do they take the bus? (No/never)
9. Does Mr. Bascomb smoke cigars? (Yes/usually)

d   *Complete the following sentences using a possessive adjective and a possessive pronoun.*

Example: Nancy brought ___*her*___ dictionary and I brought ___*mine*___.

1. They washed _____ clothes and we washed _____.

2. You drove _____ car and he drove _____.

3. Albert took _____ camera and Linda took _____.

4. I paid my bills _____ and they paid _____.

5. You painted _____ house and we painted _____.

6. He visited _____ family and I visited _____.

7. We wrote to _____ friends and they wrote to _____.

8. She found _____ pen and you found _____.

e   *Read the following sentences. Then add sentences using* **can't** *+ verbs from the list below. Use each verb only once.*

understand	listen to	call	write (to)
drink	wear	buy	drive
read	open	play	sing

Examples: I don't have her phone number. ___*I can't call her*___

           This book is boring. ___*I can't read it*___.

1. This shirt is dirty. _____

2. I don't have their address. _____

3. He's talking in Chinese. _____

4. That car isn't mine. _____

5. I don't have the key to the garage. _____

6. The guitar is broken. _____

7. She has a terrible voice. _____

8. I don't know the words to that song. _____

9. This coffee is cold. _____

10. That camera is too expensive. _____

f *Look at the pictures of Peter and make sentences about what he is doing now.*

1. **He's getting up.**

g *Make sentences about what he does every day.*

1. **He gets up.**

h *Make sentences about what he did yesterday.*

1. **He got up.**

i *Answer the following questions about yourself, using the short answer form.*

Examples: Do you often get up before eight o'clock?
Yes, I do. OR No, I don't.

Did you get up before eight o'clock this morning?
Yes, I did. OR No, I didn't.

1. Do you often make breakfast?
2. Did you make breakfast this morning?
3. Do you usually take the bus?
4. Did you take the bus yesterday?
5. Did you go to the library yesterday?

6. Did you go to the park?
7. Do you often listen to records?
8. Did you listen to records yesterday?
9. Did you watch television?

j *Complete the following sentences using suitable prepositions.*

Example: They're taking pictures ___*of*___ Miss Hackey ___*for*___ the newspapers.

1. Peter is driving _____ Los Angeles _____ San Francisco.

2. He's taking his dog _____ him.

3. Tino is taking orders _____ the Hambys.

4. Mrs. Hamby wants a bowl _____ vegetable soup _____ dinner.

5. Tino doesn't have any pictures _____ Italy _____ the wall.

6. Last summer Nancy traveled _____ the world.

7. She flew _____ some high mountains _____ South America.

8. She traveled _____ the Pacific Ocean _____ the island _____ Tahiti.

9. She stayed _____ Tahiti _____ two weeks.

k   READ AND PRACTICE

A: Excuse me. Do you sell eye shadow?

B: Yes, it's in the cosmetics department.

A: Where's the cosmetics department?

B: It's on the first floor.

C: Excuse me. Do you sell dressers?

D: Yes, they're in the furniture department.

C: Where's the furniture department?

D: It's on the third floor.

Ask and answer questions as in the dialogues above.

1. dishes
2. perfume
3. chairs

4. couches
5. lipstick
6. cups

7. cologne
8. tables
9. pans

10. lamps
11. bath soap
12. coffeepots

l   *Complete the following sentences using the simple past tense.*

Example: Tino _went_ to the florist's and _bought_ some flowers. (go/buy)

1. Barney _____ all day yesterday. (work)

2. He _____ a lot of tourists at the airport. (meet)

3. He _____ them to the Wickam Hotel. (take)

4. After work he _____ to Nick's Garage. (go)

5. His friends _____ all there. (be)

6. They _____ Coke and _____ cards. (drink/play)

7. Barney _____ every game. He never _____ . (win/lose)

8. He _____ a good time with his friends. (have)

9. Barney _____ the garage at eight-thirty. (leave)

10. He _____ in his taxi and _____ home. (get/drive)

Daisy Humple has a small apartment near the center of Wickam City. Her boyfriend, Simon, is a magician. He lives a long way from Daisy, on the other side of town. Every weekend he appears at her apartment. He usually brings her chocolates or flowers. He pulls them out of his hat. Sometimes Daisy and Simon play cards. He always wins, and Daisy thinks he is lucky. Actually, Simon never loses at cards or any other game. He is very clever, and he is also very amusing. He tells a lot of funny stories, and she always laughs. Simon and Daisy are very happy together. But they're a mysterious couple. They often disappear on weekends, and nobody knows where they go.

m   *Answer the following questions about the story.*

1. Where is Daisy's apartment?
2. What is her boyfriend's name?
3. Does he live near Daisy?
4. When does he come to her apartment?
5. What does he usually bring her?
6. Who always wins when Simon and Daisy play cards?
7. Why does Daisy always laugh when she is with Simon?
8. Why are Simon and Daisy a mysterious couple?

n   *Change the story about Simon and Daisy to the simple past tense.*

o *Look at the pictures and answer the following questions.*

  1. What's Peter going to do?
     He's going to wash the car.
  2. What are Mr. and Mrs. Bascomb going to do?
  3. What's Jack going to do?
  4. What's Anne going to do?
  5. What are Jimmy and his friends going to do?
  6. What's Barney going to do?
  7. What's Tino going to do?
  8. What are Otis and Gloria going to do?

p *Answer the following questions as indicated.*

  1. Is Peter going to wash the dishes?
     No, he isn't. He's going to wash the car.
  2. Are Mr. and Mrs. Bascomb going to eat dinner?
     Yes, they are.
  3. Is Jack going to shave?
  4. Is Anne going to call the fire department?
  5. Are Jimmy and his friends going to play tennis?
  6. Is Barney going to take a bath?
  7. Is Tino going to buy some candy?
  8. Are Otis and Gloria going to play cards?

q *Answer the following questions, using opposites.*

  Example: Does Albert eat slowly?
             No, he eats quickly.

  1. Does Jack drive carefully?   6. Does she speak loudly?
  2. Does Anne work well?   7. Does Albert run quickly?
  3. Does Mrs. Golo speak softly?   8. Does Otis dance badly?
  4. Does Fred read quickly?   9. Does Barney drive dangerously?
  5. Does Barbara work badly?

r *Give short answers to the following questions.*

  Example: You like rock music, don't you?
             Yes, I do. OR **No, I don't.**

  1. You don't have a record player, do you?
  2. You're going out tonight, aren't you?
  3. You aren't going to a movie, are you?
  4. You got up at eight o'clock this morning, didn't you?
  5. You didn't have eggs for breakfast, did you?
  6. You had a good time last night, didn't you?
  7. You weren't at home, were you?
  8. You dance very well, don't you?
  9. You don't play tennis, do you?

New York · 68°/43°

READ AND PRACTICE

A: How was the weather in New York yesterday?

B: It was rainy.

A: What was the high temperature?

B: Sixty-eight degrees.

s   *Ask and answer questions about the weather in different cities, as in the dialogue above. Use these adjectives to describe the weather:* **sunny, cloudy, rainy, snowy, windy.**

1. Rio de Janeiro · 90°/72°

2. London · 65°/46°

3. Moscow · 31°/14°

4. Paris · 69°/50°

5. Tokyo · 73°/52°

6. Jerusalem · 87°/62°

t   *Complete the following sentences as indicated:*

Example: Simon is going to Daisy's. He's taking ___*his*___ cards with ___*him*___ .

1. Linda is going to class. She's taking _____ notebook with _____ .

2. Peter is going to the movies. He's taking _____ girlfriend with _____ .

3. Our neighbors are going to the park. They're taking _____ lunch with _____ .

4. I'm going to the zoo. I'm taking _____ camera with _____ .

5. Mr. Wankie is going to Mexico. He's taking _____ wife with _____ .

6. Mrs. Golo is going to the market. She's taking _____ shopping bag with _____ .

7. We're going to the beach. We're taking _____ beach towels with _____ .

8. The Browns are going to New York. They're taking _____ children with _____ .

9. Anne is going to a party. She's taking _____ guitar with _____ .

u   *Complete the following sentences using suitable nouns. There can be more than one suitable noun for each sentence.*

Example: The bus can hold forty *passengers* .

1. I talked with Alice last night. We had an interesting _____ .

2. She isn't very pretty, but she has a good _____ .

3. Alice is married. Her _____ works at the post office.

4. He works during the day and studies in the _____ .

5. Can you get a good _____ in the public schools?

6. That's a good question, but I don't have the _____ .

7. I like Sam and Mabel. They're nice _____ _____ .

8. They're planting tomatoes in their _____ .

9. Canada is a beautiful _____ , but it gets very cold in the _____ .

10. We're going to Mexico on our next _____ .

11. I'm an American. What's your _____ ?

12. I can speak English, Spanish, and French. How many _____ can you speak?

v   *Ask and answer questions as indicated.*

Example: sing
Student A: **Can you sing?**
Student B: **Yes, but I'm not going to sing right now.**

1. dance
2. play the piano
3. ride a motorcycle
4. stand on your head
5. walk on your hands
6. do the tango
7. play the guitar
8. draw a horse
9. make a paper airplane

w   *Answer the following questions about yourself.*

1. Are you usually on time?
2. What do you say when you're late?
3. Do you wait for your friends when they're late? How long do you wait?
4. What language do you speak with your friends?
5. How often do you speak English outside of class?
6. Where did you have lunch yesterday? What did you eat?
7. How is the weather today? Do you need your umbrella? sunglasses?
8. What are you going to do after class? tonight? this weekend?
9. Do you laugh easily? Do you think people are funny?
10. How do you relax?
11. Does time pass quickly or slowly for you?
12. Do you like summer? Why?
13. Why do some people think winter is a sad time of year?

VOCABULARY

admire	disappear	lipstick	plane	than
appear	dresser	lovely	problem	thousand
			pull (v.)	together
boat	eye shadow	magician		
boring		mile	quite	voice
broken	frog legs	mountain		
	funny	mysterious	raincoat	world
candy	furniture			
clever		nobody	sail (v.)	
cologne	journey		shopping bag	
continue		ocean		
cosmetics	land (v.)		teahouse	
couple	learn	perfect	teapot	

TEST

1. Nancy traveled _____ the world.

   a. over   c. across
   b. on   d. around

2. She flew _____ high mountains.

   a. over   c. at
   b. under   d. in

3. She was _____ Paris last month.

   a. to   c. in
   b. at   d from

4. Jack asked me a lot of questions _____ my job.

   a. of   c. for
   b. about   d. on

5. Where did you go yesterday?
   I went _____ the library.

   a. at   c. for
   b. in   d. to

6. Is this typewriter _____ ?

   a. your   c. to you
   b. yours   d. you

7. The boys are washing _____ clothes.

   a. their   c. there
   b. they're   d. theirs

8. Whose car is that?
   It's _____ .

   a. her   c. hers
   b. to her   d. Mrs. Jacobs

9. I'm taking _____ some chocolates.

   a. her   c. hers
   b. to her   d. she

10. He's telling _____ an amusing story.

    a. they   c. to them
    b. them   d. their

11. Don't talk _____ .

    a. him   c. to him
    b. he   d. at him

12. _____ coffee in the pot.

    a. It's a   c. There's a
    b. It has   d. There's some

13. _____ magazines in the closet.

    a. They're   c. There's a
    b. Their   d. There are

14. _____ bottle in the sink.

    a. It's a   c. It has a
    b. There's a   d. There are

15. She _____ the bus every day.

    a. taking   c. takes
    b. is taking   d. take

16. I never _____ coffee.

    a. drink   c. drinks
    b. am drinking d. to drink

17. He _____ today.

    a. are working c. work
    b. is working   d. working

18. Look! They _____ in the street.

    a. is playing   c. play
    b. plays   d. are playing

19. Does Anne like music?
    Yes, she _____ .

    a. do   c. does
    b. likes   d. does like

20. Do they always watch television?
    Yes, they _____ .

    a. watch   c. do watch
    b. do   d. does

21. I don't need _____ money.

    a. some   c. another
    b. any   d. one

22. We bought _____ food.

    a. some   c. a
    b. any   d. one

23. She doesn't have any sugar.
    She needs _____ .

    a. any   c. some
    b. one   d. another

24. They _____ in New York last week.

    a. are   c. was
    b. went   d. were

25. Maria _____ at home yesterday.

    a. is   c. were
    b. was   d. went

26. Did she _____ that movie?

    a. go   c. see
    b. look   d. saw

27. Sam didn't _____ to the meeting.

    a. come   c. comes
    b. came   d. coming

28. He _____ home last night.

    a. stay   c. is staying
    b. stays   d. stayed

29. Did Mabel wash the dishes?
    Yes, she _____ .

    a. did   c. wash
    b. did wash   d. washed

30. Did they have chicken for dinner?
    No, they _____ .

    a. didn't have   c. have not
    b. didn't   d. don't

31. They ate _____ because they were
    in a hurry.

    a. well   c. quickly
    b. slowly   d. carefully

32. The streets are dangerous.
    Drive _____ .

    a. happily   c. accurately
    b. quickly   d. carefully

33. Gloria is a good dancer.
    She dances _____ .

    a. well   c. goodly
    b. good   d. fine

34. Otis is _____ .

    a. one artist   c. an artist
    b. a artist   d. artist

35. Are you a tourist? No, I _____ here.

    a. come   c. travel
    b. live   d. visit

36. Mrs. Golo is sick. Call a _____ .

    a. policeman   c. mechanic
    b. repairman   d. doctor

37. I'm going to the market to _____
    some milk.

    a. buy   c. drink
    b. borrow   d. have

38. You need an umbrella on _____ days.

    a. windy   c. sunny
    b. rainy   d. cloudy

39. It's always hot _____ the summer.

    a. at   c. in
    b. on   d. for

40. How was your vacation? It was _____ .

    a. wonderful   c. in Brazil
    b. two weeks   d. $1,000.00

IRREGULAR VERBS

INFINITIVE	PAST TENSE	INFINITIVE	PAST TENSE	INFINITIVE	PAST TENSE
be	was/were	give	gave	sing	sang
bring	brought	go	went	sit	sat
buy	bought	have	had	speak	spoke
come	came	hold	held	stand	stood
cut	cut	know	knew	swim	swam
do	did	leave	left	take	took
drink	drank	lose	lost	teach	taught
drive	drove	make	made	tell	told
eat	ate	meet	met	think	thought
feed	fed	put	put	understand	understood
find	found	read	read	wear	wore
fly	flew	ride	rode	win	won
forget	forgot	see	saw	write	wrote
get	got	shine	shone		

VOCABULARY

This vocabulary includes all the words used in the text, along with the number of the page on which the word appears for the first time. Nouns are given in the singular only. Verbs are given here in the infinitive form; to find the past tense of irregular verbs, see page 255.

Parts of speech have been omitted except for words that can be used as more than one part of speech. These abbreviations are used: adj. = adjective; adv. = adverb; n. = noun; prep. = preposition; v. = verb.

a, 3
about, 76
accurately, 228
across, 48
actor, 121
actress, 232
address (n.), 48
admire, 241
afraid, 59
African, 207
after, 208
afternoon, 47
ah, 42
air, 153
airplane, 14
airport, 10
all, 49
alone, 137
already, 161
also, 94
always, 133
am, 2
American, 18
amusing, 153
an, 4
and, 2
angry, 190
animal, 64
announcer, 232
another, 149
answer, 43
antique shop, 45
anxiously, 232
any, 101
anyone, 193
apartment, 88
appear, 247
appetite, 164
apple, 7
April, 195

are, 2
around, 102
art, 118
artist, 4
ask, 43
aspirin, 58
at, 10
athlete, 111
attend, 232
August, 124
author, 121
autograph, 232
away, 49
awful, 192

back (n.), 225
bad, 21
badly, 228
ball, 9
ballet, 21
banana, 130
band, 125
bank, 10
banker, 3
barber shop, 50
baseball, 111
basket, 215
basketball, 78
bath, 68
bathroom, 72
bathtub, 110
beach, 132
beautiful, 17
because, 137
bed, 110
bedroom, 110
beer, 242
before, 130
behind, 9
belong, 110

bench, 137
bicycle, 22
big, 31
bill, 60
biography, 121
bird, 7
birthday, 118
black, 29
blackboard, 36
blond, 21
boat, 240
bone, 141
book, 6
bookcase, 9
book store, 50
boot, 102
bored, 137
boring, 243
borrow, 177
bottle, 6
bowl, 103
box, 103
boy, 22
boyfriend, 96
brand-new, 24
Brazilian, 27
bread, 103
bread crumb, 137
breakfast, 76
bring, 40
broken, 243
brother, 79
brown, 86
brush (v.), 68
bucket, 175
building, 28
bum, 62
bus, 12
business, 20
businessman, 3

bus stop, 12
busy, 59
but, 85
butter, 103
butterfly, 109
buy, 78
by, 88

cafe, 100
cake, 106
calendar, 196
call (v.), 40
camera, 84
can (n.), 103
can (v.), 166
candle, 40
candy, 249
capital, 27
car, 11
card, 8
care (n.), 153
careful, 228
carefully, 228
carnation, 224
carry, 215
cartoon, 121
cashier, 71
cat, 7
catch, 175
catfish, 174
center, 153
cereal, 103
certainly, 119
chair, 6
change (v.), 179
chase (v.), 109
cheap, 22
checkers, 164
cheese, 103
cherry, 104

chess, 164
chicken, 7
chocolate, 106
church, 240
cigar, 78
cigarette, 151
city, 27
class, 37
classical, 111
classroom, 28
clean (adj.), 22
clean (v.), 75
clearly, 229
clever, 247
clock, 6
close (v.), 36
closet, 149
clothes, 160
cloudy, 190
coat, 6
Coca-Cola, 43
coffee, 68
coffeepot, 104
coffee shop, 70
Coke, 70
cold, 17
collection, 109
college, 137
cologne, 246
color, 24
come, 38
comedy, 121
company, 153
complete (v.), 61
composition, 119
concert, 224
construction, 199
continue, 240
conversation, 137
cook (n.), 164

cookie, 104
corn, 216
corner, 11
cosmetics, 246
couch, 246
counter, 74
country, 21
country singer, 21
couple, 247
cowboy, 20
cross (v.), 123
crowd, 232
cup, 41
customer, 146
cut (v.), 75

damp, 190
dance (v.), 39
dancer, 21
dangerous, 49
darts, 71
daughter, 95
day, 45
December, 118
degree, 215
delicious, 213
dental floss, 60
department
  store, 50
desk, 28
dessert, 167
detergent, 180
dictionary, 43
different, 118
dinner, 40
dirty, 22
disappear, 247
disco, 121
discuss, 199
dish, 40
do, 37
doctor, 3
dog, 7
dollar, 45
door, 39
down, 36
downtown, 137
Dr., 109
drama, 121
draw (v.), 77
dress (n.), 24

dresser, 246
drink (n.), 111
drink (v.), 70
drive (v.), 123
driver, 153
drugstore, 123
drums, 164
dry, 160
during, 138

each, 45
early, 135
easy, 137
eat, 37
economy, 199
education, 137
egg, 11
eight, 25
eighteen, 25
eighteenth, 195
eighth, 195
eighty, 44
either, 132
eleven, 25
eleventh, 195
emergency, 48
employee, 153
empty, 160
encourage, 199
encyclopedia, 79
end (v.), 206
English, 18
enjoy, 119
enter, 220
envelope, 9
establishment, 199
evening, 47
ever, 134
every, 109
everything, 83
except, 167
excite, 232
excuse (v.), 18
exercise, 179
exhibition, 118
expensive, 22
experience, 153
expert, 109
expression, 118
eye shadow, 246

face, 124
factory, 199
fall (n.), 194
family, 77
famous, 232
fantastic, 147
fat, 22
father, 40
favorite, 24
February, 195
fee, 137
feed (v.), 137
fence, 102
fifteen, 25
fifteenth, 195
fifth, 195
fifty, 44
film (n.), 232
finally, 215
find (v.), 212
fine (adj.), 2
fire (n.), 48
fire department, 48
fireman, 123
fire truck, 123
first, 118
fish (n.), 175
fisherman, 175
fishing pole, 177
five, 25
flamenco, 210
floor, 30
florist, 224
flour, 224
flower, 8
flute, 164
fly (n.), 112
follow, 232
food, 106
football, 70
for, 49
foreign, 153
forget, 60
form, 61
forty, 44
four, 25
fourteen, 25
fourteenth, 195
fourth, 195
free, 193
French, 29

French fries, 106
Friday, 195
fried (adj.), 106
friend, 20
friendly, 109
frog legs, 241
from, 19
front, 102
fruit, 64
funny, 247
furniture, 246

game (n.), 70
garage, 10
garden (n.), 94
gas, 153
gas station, 10
German, 29
get, 68
get up (v.), 59
girl, 20
girlfriend, 84
give, 52
glass, 6
glasses, 176
go, 36
good, 21
goodbye, 71
good morning, 2
grade (n.), 146
grape, 152
grass, 75
green, 80
guest, 199
guitar, 23
gun, 45

hair, 68
haircut, 179
half, 135
ham, 105
hamburger, 132
hammer, 169
hand, 252
handbag, 87
handsome, 21
happily, 232
happy, 18
hardware
  store, 169
hat, 6

have, 83
he, 3
head, 252
hello, 2
help (v.), 76
her, 5
here, 42
hers, 107
high school, 146
him, 38
his, 5
historical, 121
history, 27
hold (v.), 160
holiday, 195
home, 28
homework, 89
horse, 64
hospital, 10
hot, 17
hot dog, 123
hotel, 153
hour, 101
house, 48
housewares, 246
housewife, 40
how, 2
humility, 83
hundred, 215
hungry, 17
hurry, 49
husband, 69

I, 2
ice cream, 103
idea, 118
immediately, 49
important, 84
in, 9
include, 118
information, 153
in front of, 9
intelligent, 17
interesting, 96
invite, 224
is, 2
it, 6
Italian, 18
itinerary, 196

January, 195

quarter, 46
question, 50
quick, 228
quickly, 228
quiet, 135
quite, 241

rabbit, 7
radiator, 153
radio, 78
rain (n.), 191
raincoat, 180
rainy, 149
rat, 64
read, 50
reader, 228
ready, 40
really, 85
record (n.), 140
record player, 84
red, 24
refrigerator, 84
regular, 167
relax, 225
repair (v.), 166
repeat, 39
represent, 200
representative, 199
responsibility, 137
rest (v.), 75
restaurant, 74
return (v.), 191
rich, 17
ride (v.), 166
right, 49
rock music, 111
roof, 94
room, 37
rose, 100
ruler, 169
Russian, 21

sad, 18
safe, 202
Sagittarian, 118
sail (v.), 240
sale, 119
samba, 240
same, 160
sandwich, 42
Saturday, 132

sauce, 167
say, 71
school, 28
science fiction, 121
season, 194
second, 195
secretary, 3
see, 210
seldom, 133
September, 195
seven, 25
seventeen, 25
seventeenth, 195
seventh, 195
seventy, 44
shampoo, 162
shape (n.), 118
shave (v.), 140
she, 3
shelf, 40
shine (v.), 77
shoe, 24
shopping bag, 251
short, 21
show (n.), 234
show (v.), 118
shower, 68
sick, 177
sidewalk, 100
sign (n.), 176
sign (v.), 232
sing, 140
singer, 21
single, 29
sink (n.), 110
sir, 42
sister, 75
sit, 36
six, 25
sixteen, 25
sixteenth, 195
sixth, 195
sixty, 44
slice (n.), 106
slow, 228
slowly, 228
small, 29
smart, 175
smell (v.), 174
smile (v.), 77
smoke (v.), 77

snack, 110
snack bar, 70
snake, 64
snowy, 250
socks, 160
soft, 231
some, 100
sometimes, 133
son, 95
song, 125
sonny, 161
sorry, 213
soup, 103
spaghetti, 106
Spanish, 203
speak, 131
speaker, 228
spider, 64
sport, 111
sports car, 132
spring (n.), 194
stamp (n.), 85
stand (v.), 36
star (n.), 121
start (v.), 174
statue, 109
stay, 214
step (n.), 102
still, 169
stop (v.), 153
storekeeper, 152
story, 121
stove, 110
strange, 118
street, 48
strong, 118
student, 19
study (v.), 146
stupid, 31
subject, 137
sugar, 151
suitcase, 224
summer, 194
sun, 65
Sunday, 77
sunny, 190
supermarket, 50
swim (v.), 198

table, 6
take, 40

talk, 37
talker, 118
tall, 21
tango, 252
tank, 148
taxi, 84
taxi driver, 11
tea, 68
teacher, 28
teahouse, 241
team, 111
teapot, 180
teeth, 58
telegram, 79
telephone, 43
television, 76
tell, 147
temperature, 215
ten, 25
tennis, 146
tenth, 195
terrible, 190
than, 240
thank you, 2
that, 5
the, 10
theater, 100
their, 90
theirs, 107
them, 38
then, 225
there, 38
these, 8
they, 8
thin, 22
thing, 83
think, 77
third, 195
thirsty, 17
thirteen, 25
thirteenth, 195
thirtieth, 195
thirty, 44
this, 3
those, 8
thousand, 240
three, 25
Thursday, 195
tie (n.), 150
time, 26
tire, 153

tired, 136
to, 2
today, 75
together, 247
toilet, 110
tomato, 106
tomorrow, 224
tonight, 39
too, 5
toothpaste, 162
touch (v.), 52
tourist, 18
towel, 160
town, 153
toy, 199
traditional, 109
transportation, 202
trash, 102
travel, 190
traveler's check, 180
tree, 11
trip, 191
truck, 12
true, 119
truth, 193
Tuesday, 195
TV, 86
twelfth, 195
twelve, 25
twentieth, 195
twenty, 25
two, 25
type (v.), 166
typewriter, 86
typist, 228

ugly, 31
umbrella, 29
uncomfortable, 215
under, 9
understand, 131
unfortunately, 215
unhappy, 190
university, 28
until, 169
unusual, 118
up, 36
us, 38
use (v.), 60
useful, 153
usually, 133